I0017297

# THE ULTIMATE GUIDE TO CYBERSECURITY IN THE DIGITAL AGE

Essential Tools and Strategies to Protect Your Data and Privacy

## THOMPSON CARTER

# TABLE OF CONTENTS

# Introduction

In today's rapidly evolving digital world, cybersecurity is no longer just an IT concern but a fundamental business imperative. With every advancement in technology, cyber threats are becoming increasingly sophisticated, and the impact of cyberattacks can be devastating. As organizations and individuals rely more heavily on interconnected systems and data-driven services, the need for robust cybersecurity measures has never been more critical. The digital landscape is teeming with vulnerabilities, making it essential to stay ahead of cybercriminals and proactively protect valuable assets.

**The Ultimate Guide to Cybersecurity in the Digital Age** aims to provide readers with an in-depth understanding of modern cybersecurity, its critical importance, and the advanced tools and strategies that are shaping the future of defense. This book is not just for cybersecurity professionals but also for anyone who uses digital technologies—whether you're an individual seeking to protect personal data, a small business looking to safeguard your assets, or an executive making strategic decisions on information security.

We begin by laying a solid foundation in **the basics of cybersecurity**, explaining why protecting data and networks is a fundamental requirement in today's interconnected world. We explore key concepts such as confidentiality, integrity, and availability (the **CIA Triad**), which serve as the bedrock of every security initiative. Through **real-world case studies** and up-to-date examples, we paint a clear picture of the challenges businesses face, from ransomware attacks to insider threats and the critical role of risk management and policy development.

The journey then shifts toward **practical, hands-on strategies** that can be used to mitigate risks. You'll learn about powerful **tools and technologies**, such as AI-driven threat detection systems, machine learning-based defenses, and **blockchain**—each playing an increasingly pivotal role in revolutionizing how we protect ourselves from malicious attacks. **Penetration testing**, vulnerability assessments, and **advanced threat protection tools** are explored in depth, providing actionable insights that can be applied directly to any organization's cybersecurity framework.

One of the most important topics covered is **incident response and recovery**. We'll look at how organizations can prepare for cyberattacks before they happen, the steps involved in responding to an attack, and how to recover effectively. With cyber incidents becoming more common, having a clear, well-practiced response plan is essential for minimizing damage and ensuring business continuity.

Looking ahead, we explore **emerging technologies**, such as **quantum computing** and **next-generation encryption** systems, and how they will transform the cybersecurity landscape. These technologies have the potential to reshape how we secure data, detect threats, and manage identity in an increasingly complex and interconnected world.

Ultimately, this guide is designed to equip readers with a comprehensive understanding of cybersecurity, providing them with the knowledge and tools needed to protect themselves, their organizations, and their digital futures. Whether you are seeking to build your cybersecurity skills from the ground up or deepen your expertise in advanced technologies, this book will serve as an essential resource in your journey towards mastering cybersecurity in the digital age.

By the end of this book, you'll not only have a thorough understanding of today's cybersecurity challenges but also the skills to adapt to and stay ahead of the evolving threats that will define tomorrow's digital world.

# Chapter 1: What is Cybersecurity?

*Overview of Cybersecurity and Its Importance in the Digital Age*

Cybersecurity refers to the practices, technologies, and processes designed to protect computers, networks, programs, and data from unauthorized access, attacks, or damage. In today's interconnected world, where nearly everything is dependent on technology, cybersecurity has become a fundamental aspect of safeguarding personal, business, and governmental information. The rise of digital transformation, cloud computing, and the Internet of Things (IoT) has led to a massive increase in the volume of sensitive data stored online, making cybersecurity a critical focus for everyone.

As businesses and individuals move towards an increasingly digital world, the need to protect our digital assets has never been more urgent. Data breaches, identity theft, and cyberattacks are some of the key concerns that affect both the private and public sectors. Cybersecurity not only helps protect against these threats but also builds trust, enables secure transactions, and ensures privacy in the digital space.

*Why is Cybersecurity Important?*

1. **Data Protection:**
   - In the digital age, sensitive data—such as personal information, financial details, and intellectual property—is constantly being generated and shared.

Cybersecurity ensures that this data is kept secure from hackers and malicious entities.

2. **Business Continuity:**
   o Cybersecurity is vital for protecting business operations. Without it, companies risk losing access to crucial data, damaging their reputation, and suffering financial losses. Cyberattacks like ransomware can shut down operations for days or even weeks.

3. **Protection Against Financial Loss:**
   o Cybercrime, including identity theft, credit card fraud, and hacking into financial accounts, is a major threat. Effective cybersecurity helps prevent direct financial losses.

4. **Preserving Reputation and Trust:**
   o Businesses that experience data breaches can suffer reputational damage, leading to loss of customers and partners. Cybersecurity helps build trust by ensuring that sensitive data remains secure.

5. **Compliance and Legal Protection:**
   o Many industries are governed by strict data protection laws (e.g., GDPR in Europe, HIPAA in the healthcare industry). Effective cybersecurity helps organizations meet compliance requirements, preventing legal issues and penalties.

*The Evolving Nature of Cyber Threats*

Cyber threats are constantly evolving, becoming more sophisticated, and targeting a wider array of systems. The digital landscape has changed rapidly in recent years, and as new technologies emerge, new vulnerabilities arise. Let's explore some of the key trends and emerging threats that shape the cybersecurity landscape.

**1. Malware and Ransomware:**

- **Malware** refers to malicious software designed to harm or exploit any device, service, or network. This includes viruses, worms, and Trojans.
- **Ransomware** is a form of malware that locks users out of their systems or encrypts their files, demanding payment for the decryption key. High-profile attacks like the WannaCry ransomware attack have shown the devastating impact of these threats.

**2. Phishing and Social Engineering:**

- Phishing involves tricking individuals into revealing sensitive information (e.g., passwords, credit card details) by pretending to be a trustworthy entity.

- **Social engineering** exploits human psychology to manipulate individuals into breaking security protocols, often by exploiting their trust or fear.

## 3. Advanced Persistent Threats (APT):

- APTs are prolonged and targeted cyberattacks, typically initiated by nation-state actors or highly organized groups. These attacks are designed to infiltrate networks over extended periods, avoiding detection while stealing sensitive data or causing disruption.

## 4. Cloud Security Risks:

- As more organizations migrate to the cloud for data storage and services, the security of cloud infrastructures becomes a major concern. Poorly configured cloud services or weak authentication protocols can lead to breaches, making cloud security a top priority.

## 5. Internet of Things (IoT) Vulnerabilities:

- The growing adoption of IoT devices—such as smart home appliances, connected healthcare devices, and industrial sensors—has expanded the potential attack surface. These devices often have weak security and are vulnerable to being exploited for cyberattacks.

## 6. Artificial Intelligence (AI) in Cybersecurity:

- While AI can enhance security by detecting and responding to threats in real time, it is also being used by attackers to automate attacks and discover vulnerabilities. AI-driven attacks are capable of bypassing traditional security mechanisms, making them a major concern for cybersecurity professionals.

## 7. Supply Chain Attacks:

- In a supply chain attack, cybercriminals target a trusted third-party vendor or service provider to gain access to a larger organization's network. These attacks can be difficult to detect, as the compromised vendor may appear legitimate.

## 8. Cryptocurrency-related Attacks:

- With the rise of cryptocurrency, there has been an increase in attacks targeting digital wallets, cryptocurrency exchanges, and users holding significant amounts of digital currency. These attacks often involve phishing or exploiting vulnerabilities in blockchain technology.

---

*The Growing Need for Proactive Cybersecurity Measures*

As the nature of cyber threats continues to evolve, cybersecurity strategies must adapt accordingly. A reactive approach, where companies only respond to attacks after they occur, is no longer sufficient. Instead, proactive cybersecurity measures are essential.

1. **Regular System Updates and Patches:**
   - Keeping systems and software up to date ensures that known vulnerabilities are patched before attackers can exploit them.

2. **Employee Training and Awareness:**
   - One of the most significant security risks comes from human error. Organizations should invest in ongoing cybersecurity training to help employees recognize phishing emails, avoid unsafe practices, and understand security protocols.

3. **Multi-layered Security:**
   - Implementing multiple layers of security (e.g., firewalls, intrusion detection systems, and encryption) reduces the likelihood that an attacker will successfully breach a network.

4. **Data Encryption and Backup:**
   - Encrypting sensitive data ensures that even if an attacker gains access to it, they cannot read or use it. Regular backups also ensure that data can be restored in the event of a ransomware attack or data breach.

5. **Incident Response Planning:**

o Having an incident response plan in place ensures that, in the event of a breach, the organization can quickly contain the threat, minimize damage, and recover systems with minimal disruption.

---

Cybersecurity is not just the responsibility of IT departments—it is a shared responsibility that affects all individuals and organizations. As cyber threats continue to evolve and become more sophisticated, the need for robust security measures is more urgent than ever. By understanding the nature of these threats and implementing proactive security strategies, individuals and organizations can protect their data, preserve their privacy, and ensure the integrity of their digital lives in this increasingly connected world.

# Chapter 2: Types of Cyber Threats

## *Overview*

In the digital age, cyber threats are pervasive and constantly evolving. They target both individuals and organizations, seeking to exploit vulnerabilities for financial gain, intellectual property theft, espionage, or other malicious purposes. This chapter delves into some of the most common types of cyber threats, including malware, phishing, ransomware, and data breaches. We will also explore high-profile case studies of cyberattacks to understand how these threats unfold in the real world.

---

## 1. Malware

### *What is Malware?*

Malware (malicious software) refers to any software intentionally designed to cause damage or disrupt normal operations on a computer, network, or device. Malware can take many forms, including viruses, worms, spyware, trojans, and more.

### *Common Types of Malware:*

- **Virus:** A piece of code that attaches itself to a legitimate program and spreads to other files or systems.

- **Worm:** A self-replicating malware that spreads independently, often over a network.
- **Trojan Horse:** Disguised as legitimate software, a trojan opens the door for other malware or unauthorized access.
- **Spyware:** A type of malware designed to gather personal information without the user's consent.
- **Adware:** Malware that delivers unwanted advertisements, often through pop-ups or redirecting web traffic.

### Example: The Stuxnet Worm

One of the most sophisticated malware attacks, Stuxnet was a computer worm discovered in 2010. It targeted industrial control systems and was designed to disrupt Iran's nuclear program by causing damage to centrifuges used for uranium enrichment. It was a highly targeted attack, likely attributed to state actors.

## 2. Phishing

### What is Phishing?

Phishing is a type of cyberattack where attackers deceive individuals into revealing sensitive information, such as passwords, credit card numbers, or personal details, by pretending to be a trustworthy entity. Phishing attacks typically come in the form of emails, messages, or fake websites that appear legitimate.

*Common Phishing Techniques:*

- **Email Phishing:** Fraudulent emails claiming to be from a trusted organization, asking the recipient to click on a link or download an attachment.
- **Spear Phishing:** A more targeted form of phishing, where attackers personalize emails to specific individuals or organizations to increase the likelihood of success.
- **Whaling:** A type of spear phishing targeted at high-level executives, where the attacker impersonates a trusted business partner or organization.
- **Smishing (SMS Phishing):** Phishing attempts carried out through text messages or SMS.

*Example: The 2016 Democratic National Committee (DNC) Email Breach*

In 2016, the DNC suffered a major cyberattack when hackers gained access to their email system through a spear-phishing campaign. The attack resulted in the theft and public release of sensitive political documents, which influenced the U.S. presidential election. This attack highlighted the effectiveness of phishing in compromising sensitive information.

## 3. Ransomware

*What is Ransomware?*

Ransomware is a form of malicious software that encrypts a victim's files or locks them out of their system. The attacker then demands a ransom in exchange for restoring access to the encrypted data or system. Ransomware attacks often target businesses, healthcare institutions, and government organizations.

*How Ransomware Works:*

1. **Infection:** The victim clicks on a malicious email link, downloads a compromised file, or visits an infected website.
2. **Encryption:** The ransomware encrypts files on the victim's system, rendering them inaccessible.
3. **Ransom Demand:** A ransom note appears, demanding payment (usually in cryptocurrency) in exchange for the decryption key.

*Example: The WannaCry Ransomware Attack*

In May 2017, the WannaCry ransomware spread rapidly across the globe, affecting hundreds of thousands of computers in over 150 countries. It exploited a vulnerability in Microsoft Windows (specifically, the EternalBlue exploit, which was originally developed by the NSA). The attack impacted hospitals, businesses, and government agencies. Despite efforts to stop the attack, it caused billions of dollars in damage and served as a wake-up call for the need for better patch management and vulnerability monitoring.

## 4. Data Breaches

### *What is a Data Breach?*

A data breach occurs when unauthorized individuals gain access to confidential data, such as customer information, financial records, intellectual property, or personal details. Data breaches can result from hacking, insider threats, or poor data protection practices.

### *Common Causes of Data Breaches:*

- **Hacking:** Cybercriminals exploiting vulnerabilities to gain unauthorized access to systems or databases.
- **Phishing:** Attackers tricking individuals into disclosing their login credentials, which are then used to access data.
- **Insider Threats:** Employees or contractors intentionally or unintentionally leaking sensitive data.
- **Weak Security Practices:** Insufficient encryption, lack of access control, or outdated software that makes systems vulnerable to attack.

### *Example: The 2013 Target Data Breach*

In 2013, retailer Target suffered one of the largest data breaches in history. Hackers gained access to Target's network through a third-party vendor and were able to steal personal information, including credit and debit card details, of approximately 40 million customers. The breach led to significant financial losses for Target, as well as a damaged reputation and regulatory scrutiny.

## 5. Case Studies of High-Profile Cyberattacks

### 5.1 The Equifax Data Breach (2017)

- **Attack Details:** Hackers exploited a vulnerability in the Apache Struts framework used by Equifax, a major credit reporting agency. The breach exposed personal information, including Social Security numbers, birth dates, addresses, and driver's license numbers, of approximately 147 million Americans.
- **Impact:** The breach led to a massive public outcry, legal action, and regulatory scrutiny. Equifax was fined $700 million as part of a settlement.
- **Lessons Learned:** Regular patching of software vulnerabilities and robust network segmentation are key strategies to mitigate similar risks.

### 5.2 The Sony Pictures Hack (2014)

- **Attack Details:** A group of hackers, believed to be associated with North Korea, breached Sony Pictures' internal network, stealing sensitive data, including unreleased films, personal emails, and employee information.
- **Impact:** The hack resulted in the leak of confidential data, damage to Sony's reputation, and significant financial costs related to remediation efforts.
- **Lessons Learned:** The attack highlighted the need for stronger security measures for corporate networks and the importance of monitoring for insider threats.

### 5.3 The Colonial Pipeline Ransomware Attack (2021)

- **Attack Details:** The Colonial Pipeline, a major U.S. fuel supplier, was attacked by the DarkSide ransomware group. The hackers demanded a ransom in exchange for unlocking the company's encrypted data, disrupting fuel delivery across the Eastern U.S. for several days.
- **Impact:** The attack led to fuel shortages, panic buying, and a significant loss in revenue for Colonial Pipeline. The U.S. government intervened to secure the ransom payment.
- **Lessons Learned:** This attack demonstrated the vulnerabilities of critical infrastructure and the importance of cybersecurity for operational technology systems.

## 6.

Understanding the various types of cyber threats is essential for developing effective strategies to protect personal, business, and governmental data. As cyberattacks continue to grow in sophistication, it's crucial to stay informed and proactive in safeguarding digital assets. Case studies from high-profile cyberattacks highlight the importance of strong security measures and prompt responses to mitigate the potential impact of these threats.

# Chapter 3: The Importance of Data Protection

*Overview*

In the digital age, data is an invaluable asset, both for individuals and businesses. From personal information to proprietary business data, the safeguarding of this data has become a top priority. Cyberattacks, data breaches, and unauthorized access can lead to significant financial, reputational, and legal consequences. This chapter explores why safeguarding personal and business data is essential and outlines the key principles of data privacy and protection.

---

## 1. Why Safeguarding Personal and Business Data is Essential

### *1.1 The Value of Personal Data*

Personal data includes any information that can be used to identify an individual, such as names, addresses, phone numbers, Social Security numbers, and financial information. The value of this data has increased exponentially as individuals and organizations conduct more transactions, share personal details, and store information online. Cybercriminals recognize this value and often target personal data for theft, leading to issues such as:

- **Identity Theft:** Criminals use stolen personal information to impersonate individuals, open fraudulent accounts, or make unauthorized purchases.

- **Financial Loss:** Personal data can be used to drain bank accounts, gain access to credit cards, or steal funds.

- **Reputation Damage:** A compromised personal data breach can harm an individual's personal reputation and lead to emotional and financial distress.

## *1.2 The Value of Business Data*

For businesses, data represents more than just information—it is a key resource for growth, innovation, and competitive advantage. Critical business data includes customer details, financial records, intellectual property, employee information, and proprietary technology. The theft or loss of business data can lead to several consequences:

- **Financial Loss:** Data breaches can result in direct financial loss, fines, and the cost of remediation efforts. In fact, the cost of a data breach continues to rise, reaching millions of dollars for some organizations.

- **Intellectual Property Theft:** Losing proprietary data, such as patents, designs, or trade secrets, can be catastrophic for a business, especially if competitors or cybercriminals gain access to it.

- **Reputational Damage:** Customers and partners expect businesses to protect their data. A breach can lead to the loss of trust, damaged relationships, and a decline in sales and customers.

- **Legal Consequences:** Businesses are often required by law to protect sensitive data. Failure to do so can result in lawsuits, fines, and regulatory action, such as violations of data protection laws like GDPR, CCPA, or HIPAA.

### *1.3 Increasing Frequency of Data Breaches*

The frequency of data breaches and cyberattacks is growing. High-profile incidents, such as the 2017 Equifax breach, have shown the immense impact on individuals and businesses when sensitive data is compromised. Data breaches are often costly and difficult to recover from, which underscores the need for robust data protection strategies.

## 2. Key Principles of Data Privacy and Protection

Data protection is not just about installing software or encryption tools—it involves a holistic approach to managing and securing data at all stages, from collection to storage and disposal. Below are the key principles that should guide any data protection strategy.

### *2.1 Data Minimization*

**Principle:** Only collect the data that is necessary for a specific purpose and avoid over-collection.

- **Why it's Important:** The more data an organization collects, the greater the risk of that data being exposed or misused. By limiting data collection to only what is necessary, organizations reduce their exposure to potential breaches or misuse.
- **Real-World Example:** If a company is collecting customer data for a newsletter, it should only ask for the essential information, such as email addresses, rather than unnecessary details like phone numbers or home addresses.

## 2.2 Data Encryption

**Principle:** Encrypt sensitive data both in transit (while being transferred) and at rest (when stored).

- **Why it's Important:** Encryption ensures that even if data is intercepted or accessed by unauthorized individuals, it remains unreadable and unusable without the proper decryption keys. It is a critical safeguard for protecting sensitive business and personal data.
- **Real-World Example:** Banks and financial institutions use encryption to secure customer account information and transactions, ensuring that sensitive data cannot be exposed to cybercriminals during transfers.

## 2.3 Data Access Control

**Principle:** Ensure that access to sensitive data is restricted to authorized individuals only.

- **Why it's Important:** Implementing strong access control mechanisms prevents unauthorized individuals, including insiders, from accessing sensitive data. Role-based access control (RBAC) is a common method used to enforce the principle of least privilege, where users are given only the minimum access required to perform their job functions.
- **Real-World Example:** In a healthcare organization, access to patient data should be restricted to doctors and healthcare providers directly involved in the patient's care, while administrative staff should have limited access.

## 2.4 Regular Data Audits and Monitoring

**Principle:** Conduct regular audits and continuously monitor data usage and access logs.

- **Why it's Important:** Regular audits help identify unusual access patterns, unauthorized access, or potential security gaps in data handling. Continuous monitoring can detect and mitigate threats in real time.
- **Real-World Example:** Many large corporations use Security Information and Event Management (SIEM) systems to monitor their networks and databases for any

suspicious activity, enabling them to respond quickly to potential security incidents.

## 2.5 Data Retention and Disposal

**Principle:** Keep data only for as long as necessary and securely dispose of data when it is no longer needed.

- **Why it's Important:** Keeping unnecessary data increases the risk of it being exposed or breached. Proper disposal of data ensures that old records cannot be recovered or misused.
- **Real-World Example:** Businesses must securely dispose of old employee records or outdated customer information, ensuring that hard drives are wiped and sensitive data is erased permanently.

## 2.6 Transparency and Consent

**Principle:** Ensure that individuals are aware of how their data is being used and obtain their consent.

- **Why it's Important:** Transparency and consent are essential aspects of data privacy. People have the right to know what data is being collected and how it will be used. Businesses should implement clear privacy policies and obtain explicit consent before collecting or processing personal data.
- **Real-World Example:** Online services like social media platforms or email providers usually ask for consent before

collecting user data and provide privacy settings to allow users to manage what information they share.

---

## 3. Data Protection Laws and Regulations

Data protection is not only about technical safeguards but also about adhering to legal and regulatory requirements that govern how data should be handled. Some of the most well-known data protection laws include:

- **General Data Protection Regulation (GDPR):** A regulation by the European Union that aims to protect the privacy and personal data of EU citizens. It mandates that companies collect, process, and store personal data securely and transparently.
- **California Consumer Privacy Act (CCPA):** A privacy law that gives residents of California rights over their personal data, including the right to access, delete, and opt-out of the sale of their personal information.
- **Health Insurance Portability and Accountability Act (HIPAA):** U.S. legislation that provides data privacy and security provisions to safeguard personal health information (PHI).

*Compliance with these laws is essential for businesses to avoid penalties and legal issues related to data misuse. Implementing strong data protection practices ensures that organizations can meet these regulatory requirements and protect the privacy of their users.*

## 4.

Data protection is critical in the digital age, where cyber threats are rampant and the consequences of data breaches can be devastating. By adopting the key principles of data privacy—such as data minimization, encryption, access control, and transparency—both individuals and businesses can ensure the safety of sensitive information. Whether it's protecting personal data from cybercriminals or ensuring compliance with regulatory standards, effective data protection strategies are the foundation of trust and security in the digital world.

# Chapter 4: Cybersecurity Laws and Regulations

## Overview

In the digital age, data protection laws and regulations are essential to ensure that personal and business data are handled responsibly. These laws are designed to safeguard privacy, protect sensitive information, and ensure that organizations are held accountable for the data they collect. In this chapter, we will explore key data protection laws such as the General Data Protection Regulation (GDPR), the California Consumer Privacy Act (CCPA), and others, and examine how these laws affect both businesses and individuals.

## 1. General Data Protection Regulation (GDPR)

### What is GDPR?

The General Data Protection Regulation (GDPR) is a comprehensive data protection law that applies to all companies operating within the European Union (EU), as well as any company outside of the EU that processes data of EU citizens. GDPR was enacted in May 2018 to harmonize data privacy laws across Europe and protect the privacy and data of EU residents.

### Key Principles of GDPR:

1. **Data Subject Rights:**
   o **Right to Access:** Individuals can request access to the personal data companies hold about them.
   o **Right to Rectification:** Individuals can correct any inaccurate or incomplete data.
   o **Right to Erasure (Right to be Forgotten):** Individuals can request that their personal data be deleted in certain circumstances.
   o **Right to Data Portability:** Individuals can transfer their personal data from one service provider to another.
   o **Right to Object:** Individuals can object to the processing of their data under certain conditions.
2. **Lawful Basis for Processing:**
   o Organizations must have a lawful reason to process personal data. These include obtaining consent, fulfilling contracts, or complying with legal obligations.
3. **Data Minimization and Purpose Limitation:**
   o Data collected should be limited to what is necessary for the specific purpose, and it should not be used for other, unrelated purposes.
4. **Data Protection by Design and by Default:**
   o Organizations must implement security measures from the beginning of a project or system (data

protection by design) and ensure that only necessary data is processed by default (data protection by default).

## How GDPR Affects Businesses:

- **Data Breach Notification:** Businesses must notify authorities and affected individuals within 72 hours if there is a data breach that impacts personal data.
- **Fines and Penalties:** Organizations that fail to comply with GDPR may face hefty fines, up to 4% of global revenue or €20 million (whichever is higher).
- **Data Protection Officer (DPO):** Some organizations are required to appoint a Data Protection Officer to oversee GDPR compliance.

## How GDPR Affects Individuals:

- **Enhanced Privacy Rights:** Individuals have more control over their personal data, including the ability to access, delete, and port their data.
- **Transparency and Consent:** Individuals must be clearly informed about how their data is being used, and explicit consent must be obtained for processing.

## 2. California Consumer Privacy Act (CCPA)

*What is CCPA?*

The California Consumer Privacy Act (CCPA) is a data privacy law that applies to businesses operating in California or collecting data from California residents. Enacted in 2020, the CCPA gives California residents greater control over their personal data and how it is used by companies.

*Key Features of CCPA:*

1. **Right to Know:** California residents can request information about the personal data a business collects, the sources of that data, and the purpose for its use.
2. **Right to Delete:** Individuals can request that a business delete their personal data, with some exceptions (e.g., for legal or security purposes).
3. **Right to Opt-Out:** Individuals can opt-out of the sale of their personal data to third parties.
4. **Non-Discrimination:** Businesses are prohibited from discriminating against individuals who exercise their rights under the CCPA, such as denying services or charging different prices.

*How CCPA Affects Businesses:*

- **Data Collection Practices:** Businesses must provide clear and accessible privacy policies, informing customers about the data they collect and how it will be used.
- **Opt-Out Mechanism:** Businesses must provide a "Do Not Sell My Personal Information" option on their websites, allowing customers to opt out of the sale of their data.
- **Penalties for Non-Compliance:** The CCPA imposes fines of up to $2,500 per violation and up to $7,500 per intentional violation.

### *How CCPA Affects Individuals:*

- **Greater Control Over Data:** Individuals in California have more transparency and control over their personal data, including the ability to access, delete, and opt out of data sales.
- **Right to Sue:** Individuals can sue businesses for certain violations of the CCPA, particularly if their data is exposed in a breach due to negligence.

---

# 3. Health Insurance Portability and Accountability Act (HIPAA)

### *What is HIPAA?*

The Health Insurance Portability and Accountability Act (HIPAA) is a U.S. law that mandates the protection and confidential handling of medical information. HIPAA applies to healthcare providers, insurers, and organizations that handle patient data.

*Key Aspects of HIPAA:*

- **Privacy Rule:** Establishes national standards for the protection of health information, ensuring that individuals' medical records are kept private.
- **Security Rule:** Requires healthcare organizations to implement safeguards to protect electronic health records (EHRs) and other electronic data.
- **Breach Notification Rule:** Mandates that individuals be notified within 60 days if their protected health information is breached.

*How HIPAA Affects Businesses:*

- **Compliance Requirements:** Healthcare organizations must implement physical, administrative, and technical safeguards to protect sensitive health data.
- **Penalties for Violations:** Fines for non-compliance range from $100 to $50,000 per violation, with an annual maximum of $1.5 million.

*How HIPAA Affects Individuals:*

- **Confidentiality of Health Data:** HIPAA ensures that an individual's health information is protected and not disclosed without their consent, except under specific circumstances.
- **Right to Access Records:** Individuals have the right to access their own health records and request corrections.

## 4. General Data Protection Laws (GDPR, CCPA, HIPAA) Comparison

| Aspect | GDPR | CCPA | HIPAA |
|---|---|---|---|
| **Applicable Region** | European Union (EU) | California, USA | United States (Healthcare) |
| **Type of Data Covered** | Personal data of EU residents | Personal data of California residents | Health-related personal data |
| **Right to Access** | Yes | Yes | Yes |
| **Right to Delete** | Yes | Yes | Limited to health data |
| **Right to Opt-Out** | No | Yes (sale of personal data) | Not applicable |

| Aspect | GDPR | CCPA | HIPAA |
|---|---|---|---|
| Penalties for Non-Compliance | Up to €20 million or 4% of global revenue | Up to $7,500 per violation | Up to $50,000 per violation |

# 5. Other Key Data Protection Laws

## 5.1 The Personal Data Protection Act (PDPA)

The PDPA is Singapore's data protection law, which regulates the collection, use, and disclosure of personal data. It aims to balance the need for data protection with the use of personal data for business operations.

## 5.2 The Privacy Act (Australia)

The Privacy Act governs the collection and use of personal information in Australia. It includes principles for data collection, use, and disclosure, and provides individuals with rights to access and correct their data.

## 5.3 The Federal Information Security Modernization Act (FISMA)

FISMA is a U.S. federal law that requires government agencies and contractors to secure information systems. It establishes mandatory guidelines for the security of sensitive government data.

## 6.

Cybersecurity laws and regulations are critical in today's digital environment, where vast amounts of personal, financial, and business data are collected, stored, and processed. Laws such as GDPR, CCPA, and HIPAA provide clear frameworks to ensure data privacy and protection, holding organizations accountable for maintaining robust security practices. As data privacy concerns continue to rise, understanding these laws is essential for businesses to avoid penalties and for individuals to protect their personal information.

# Chapter 5: Confidentiality, Integrity, and Availability (CIA Triad)

## Overview

The CIA Triad—Confidentiality, Integrity, and Availability—is the foundational model for understanding and implementing security principles in cybersecurity. These three concepts form the core of any robust cybersecurity framework, ensuring that information is kept secure and accessible to authorized parties while being protected from unauthorized access and tampering. This chapter takes a deep dive into each of the principles of the CIA Triad and discusses how these principles can be applied in real-world scenarios.

---

## 1. Confidentiality

### What is Confidentiality?

Confidentiality refers to the principle of ensuring that sensitive information is only accessible to those who are authorized to view it. This is crucial for protecting personal data, business secrets, intellectual property, and sensitive government information. Maintaining confidentiality means preventing unauthorized access, disclosure, or exposure of data.

*Key Methods to Ensure Confidentiality:*

1. **Encryption:** Encrypting data ensures that even if unauthorized individuals gain access to the data, they cannot read it without the decryption key. Both data at rest (stored data) and data in transit (data being transferred over the network) should be encrypted.

   o **Example:** When sending an email containing sensitive financial information, encryption ensures that only the intended recipient can read the email, preventing anyone who intercepts it from gaining access to the contents.

2. **Access Control:** Only authorized individuals should have access to sensitive data. This can be controlled using techniques such as role-based access control (RBAC), which assigns access rights based on the user's role within an organization.

   o **Example:** In a company, only HR staff should have access to employee records, while the IT department may only have access to network-related data.

3. **Authentication:** Strong authentication methods such as passwords, biometrics, or multi-factor authentication (MFA) are used to ensure that individuals accessing sensitive information are who they say they are.

   o **Example:** A financial institution requires customers to log in using a password and a one-time code sent to their mobile device to access their bank account online.

4. **Data Masking and Tokenization:** Data masking involves obfuscating sensitive data so that unauthorized individuals cannot access it in a readable format. Tokenization replaces sensitive data with an equivalent but non-sensitive placeholder.

   o **Example:** Masking the last four digits of a credit card number on a website to prevent exposure while still allowing users to recognize their account.

*Real-World Application of Confidentiality:*

In the healthcare industry, ensuring confidentiality is paramount for protecting patient information. Laws such as the Health Insurance Portability and Accountability Act (HIPAA) mandate that patient records must be kept confidential. Healthcare providers use encryption to secure patient data and ensure that only authorized personnel can access it, protecting sensitive medical histories and treatment plans from unauthorized individuals.

## 2. Integrity

*What is Integrity?*

Integrity refers to the assurance that information is accurate, complete, and unaltered from its original state. It is critical for ensuring that data is not tampered with during storage, processing, or transmission. Maintaining data integrity ensures that the information used for decision-making is reliable and trustworthy.

### *Key Methods to Ensure Integrity:*

1. **Hashing:** Hashing is a process that transforms data into a fixed-size string of characters, which is a unique representation of the original data. Hashes are used to check if data has been altered or tampered with.
   - **Example:** When downloading a software update, the website provides a hash value for the file. After downloading, the user can hash the file locally and compare it to the provided hash to ensure the file hasn't been corrupted or tampered with.
2. **Digital Signatures:** Digital signatures are cryptographic techniques used to verify the authenticity of a message or document. A digital signature ensures that the data has not been altered and confirms the sender's identity.
   - **Example:** When a lawyer sends an electronic contract to a client, they may use a digital signature to ensure the document has not been modified since it was signed.
3. **Checksums:** A checksum is a small-sized piece of data derived from a larger set of data and is used to verify the integrity of data during transmission. If the checksum doesn't

match when the data is received, it indicates that the data has been altered.

- o **Example:** When transferring a file over the internet, the file's checksum is computed and compared upon arrival to verify that the file has not been corrupted or altered during the transfer process.

4. **Version Control Systems:** These systems track changes to data over time, allowing users to see if any modifications have been made and to restore previous versions if necessary.

- o **Example:** In software development, tools like Git allow developers to track changes to code, ensuring that they can revert to a previous version of the codebase if errors or unintended changes occur.

### *Real-World Application of Integrity:*

In financial systems, integrity is critical to maintaining the accuracy of transactions. Banks use hashing and digital signatures to ensure the integrity of financial transactions, preventing fraud and ensuring that all account transfers are legitimate and unaltered during the transfer process.

---

## 3. Availability

### *What is Availability?*

Availability ensures that data and services are accessible to authorized users when they need it. This principle is about ensuring the functionality of systems, applications, and networks under normal and adverse conditions, ensuring minimal downtime and business continuity.

### *Key Methods to Ensure Availability:*

1. **Redundancy:** Redundant systems and backups help ensure that if one system fails, another system or backup can take over, ensuring minimal disruption.
   - o **Example:** A cloud service provider may use multiple data centers across different geographic locations to ensure that if one data center experiences a failure, another can take over, minimizing downtime.

2. **Disaster Recovery (DR) and Business Continuity Planning (BCP):** Disaster recovery plans ensure that businesses can recover from catastrophic events such as cyberattacks or natural disasters. Business continuity planning ensures that critical business functions continue in the event of a disaster.
   - o **Example:** A hospital has a disaster recovery plan to quickly restore access to patient records and essential services in the event of a cyberattack or system failure.

3. **Load Balancing:** Load balancing distributes network traffic or workloads across multiple servers, preventing any single server from becoming overwhelmed and ensuring consistent availability.

   o **Example:** E-commerce websites use load balancing to distribute traffic across multiple servers, ensuring that the site remains available even during high traffic periods like Black Friday sales.

4. **Patch Management:** Regularly applying security patches and updates to systems and software ensures that vulnerabilities are fixed, preventing attackers from exploiting known flaws to compromise availability.

   o **Example:** A company regularly applies patches to its web server software to prevent attackers from exploiting known vulnerabilities that could lead to server downtime.

*Real-World Application of Availability:*

In online banking systems, ensuring availability is critical. Banks invest heavily in redundant servers, backup systems, and disaster recovery processes to ensure that customers can access their accounts, make transfers, and perform transactions at any time. If the banking platform is down for even a short period, it can result in significant financial losses and loss of trust from customers.

## 4. The CIA Triad in Real-World Scenarios

### *Example 1: E-Commerce Website*

For an e-commerce website:

- **Confidentiality** ensures that customer payment information is encrypted and accessible only to authorized personnel.
- **Integrity** guarantees that product details, inventory levels, and customer orders are accurate and unaltered during processing.
- **Availability** ensures that the website remains online and functional, even during high traffic times like sales events or holidays.

### *Example 2: Government Data*

For a government agency handling sensitive citizen information:

- **Confidentiality** ensures that personal identification information (PII) is protected from unauthorized access, ensuring privacy.
- **Integrity** ensures that citizen records, tax data, and legal information are accurate and have not been tampered with.
- **Availability** ensures that essential services, such as access to records or processing applications, remain available to authorized individuals during critical times, like elections or tax season.

# 5.

The CIA Triad—Confidentiality, Integrity, and Availability—is the cornerstone of cybersecurity. Together, these principles form a robust framework that helps protect data and systems from unauthorized access, modification, and disruption. By understanding and implementing these principles, organizations can better safeguard their information, ensure operational continuity, and build trust with customers, partners, and stakeholders.

# Chapter 6: Risk Management in Cybersecurity

*Overview*

Risk management is a critical aspect of cybersecurity, as it involves identifying, assessing, and prioritizing risks to protect valuable assets and mitigate potential threats. By understanding the concepts of risk assessment and implementing effective mitigation strategies, organizations can strengthen their defenses and ensure business continuity. This chapter delves into how organizations can assess and manage cybersecurity risks, and provides guidance on identifying and prioritizing threats to protect data, systems, and networks.

## 1. Understanding Risk Assessment in Cybersecurity

Risk assessment is the process of identifying, evaluating, and analyzing potential risks that could harm an organization's cybersecurity posture. It helps organizations determine which vulnerabilities or threats pose the greatest danger to their assets and provides a framework for making informed decisions about how to address those risks.

*Key Steps in Risk Assessment:*

1. **Identify Assets:**
   - Before assessing risks, it's essential to identify the organization's valuable assets, such as intellectual property, customer data, financial information, and critical infrastructure. Each asset must be considered in terms of its importance and the potential consequences of its loss or compromise.

2. **Identify Threats and Vulnerabilities:**
   - **Threats** are potential dangers that could exploit vulnerabilities in an organization's systems or processes. These can come from external sources (e.g., hackers, natural disasters) or internal sources (e.g., employees, human error).
   - **Vulnerabilities** are weaknesses in systems, processes, or controls that can be exploited by threats to cause damage or loss.

3. **Assess the Likelihood of Risks:**
   - The next step is to assess how likely a threat is to exploit a vulnerability. This involves considering historical data, threat intelligence, and other contextual factors that can inform the likelihood of a risk materializing.

4. **Evaluate the Impact:**
   - For each identified risk, evaluate the potential impact on the organization if the risk were to occur. This

could include financial losses, reputational damage, legal consequences, or loss of customer trust. It's important to understand both the direct and indirect effects of a cyberattack or data breach.

5. **Risk Rating:**
   o Risks should be rated based on their likelihood and impact. This can be done using a risk matrix, which categorizes risks into levels (e.g., high, medium, low) to help prioritize them for mitigation.

6. **Risk Treatment:**
   o Once risks are assessed, appropriate mitigation strategies should be devised. These strategies can include reducing the likelihood of the risk, minimizing the impact, or transferring the risk (e.g., through insurance).

*Risk Assessment Tools and Techniques:*

- **Risk Matrix:** A visual tool used to map the likelihood and impact of risks on a grid to prioritize mitigation efforts.
- **Threat Modeling:** A structured approach to identifying potential threats to systems and networks and designing countermeasures.
- **Vulnerability Scanning:** Tools that automatically scan systems for known vulnerabilities and weaknesses.

- **Penetration Testing:** A simulated attack on an organization's network or systems to identify vulnerabilities and test security measures.

---

## 2. Mitigation Strategies for Cybersecurity Risks

Mitigation strategies are the actions an organization takes to reduce or eliminate the potential impact of cybersecurity risks. Effective mitigation involves implementing appropriate controls, monitoring systems, and adopting best practices to safeguard assets and ensure business continuity.

*Key Mitigation Strategies:*

1. **Implementing Strong Access Controls:**
   - Access control mechanisms such as multi-factor authentication (MFA), role-based access control (RBAC), and least privilege policies can help limit the exposure of sensitive data and reduce the risk of unauthorized access.
   - **Example:** Limiting access to critical business systems to only those employees who need it for their job functions, and requiring MFA for accessing financial systems.
2. **Encryption of Sensitive Data:**

o Encrypting data both at rest (stored data) and in transit (data being transferred over networks) ensures that even if the data is intercepted, it cannot be read or used without the decryption key.

o **Example:** A company encrypts customer data stored in databases and also ensures that data transmitted through its online portal is encrypted via SSL/TLS.

3. **Regular Software and System Updates:**

o Vulnerabilities in software are commonly exploited by cybercriminals. Keeping all software, operating systems, and applications up to date with the latest security patches is crucial in reducing the attack surface.

o **Example:** An organization sets up an automated patch management system to ensure that security patches are applied to all systems within 24 hours of their release.

4. **Firewalls and Intrusion Detection Systems (IDS):**

o Firewalls and IDS are essential in preventing unauthorized access to a network and monitoring network traffic for suspicious activity. These tools act as barriers against attacks from external and internal sources.

o **Example:** An enterprise uses a next-generation firewall and deploys an IDS to monitor network traffic and block potential attacks such as DDoS (Distributed Denial of Service).

5. **Employee Training and Awareness:**
   o Human error is a significant factor in many cyberattacks. Regular cybersecurity training can help employees recognize threats like phishing emails, avoid risky behaviors, and follow best practices for data protection.
   o **Example:** A company runs monthly cybersecurity awareness workshops for employees to help them identify phishing scams and practice safe online behavior.

6. **Backup and Disaster Recovery Plans:**
   o Ensuring that data is regularly backed up and that a disaster recovery plan is in place can help organizations recover quickly from a cyberattack or natural disaster. Having a secure backup ensures that critical data can be restored if it is lost or corrupted.
   o **Example:** A business backs up its data to an off-site cloud storage service and tests its disaster recovery plan annually to ensure minimal downtime in case of a cyberattack.

7. **Incident Response Plan:**
   o An incident response plan outlines the steps to be taken in the event of a cyberattack. It includes roles

and responsibilities, communication strategies, and actions to contain, investigate, and recover from the attack.

o **Example:** A company has a well-documented incident response plan that is tested quarterly. The plan includes steps for isolating compromised systems, notifying stakeholders, and conducting a post-incident review.

## 3. How to Identify and Prioritize Cybersecurity Risks

Identifying and prioritizing cybersecurity risks is crucial for focusing resources on the most significant threats and vulnerabilities. The risk management process should be continuous, as new risks and threats emerge over time.

*Steps to Identify Cybersecurity Risks:*

1. **Conduct a Risk Assessment:**
   o Perform a thorough risk assessment to identify the organization's critical assets, evaluate potential threats, and understand the vulnerabilities that could be exploited.

2. **Gather Threat Intelligence:**

o Use threat intelligence tools to gather information about emerging cyber threats. This could include data on new malware strains, known attack vectors, or vulnerabilities in widely used software.

3. **Monitor Network Traffic and Logs:**

o Continuous monitoring of network traffic and system logs can help detect early signs of an attack. This includes unusual behavior such as unexpected login attempts, large data transfers, or unauthorized access to sensitive files.

4. **Engage with Employees:**

o Employees are often the first line of defense against cyber threats. Regularly solicit feedback from staff regarding potential risks they may have noticed and encourage them to report suspicious activity.

*Steps to Prioritize Cybersecurity Risks:*

1. **Assess Likelihood and Impact:**

o Prioritize risks based on the likelihood of their occurrence and the potential impact they would have on the organization. High-likelihood, high-impact risks should be addressed first.

2. **Use a Risk Matrix:**

o A risk matrix is a tool that helps visualize and prioritize risks. It plots the likelihood of a risk against its potential impact, categorizing risks as high, medium, or low priority.

3. **Cost-Benefit Analysis:**
   o When deciding which risks to prioritize, consider the cost of mitigating a risk versus the potential impact of a security breach. In some cases, it may be more cost-effective to address higher-priority risks, even if they are not the most likely to occur.

4. **Focus on Critical Systems:**
   o Prioritize cybersecurity measures for the organization's most critical systems, such as customer databases, financial systems, and proprietary intellectual property. These systems often hold the most valuable and sensitive data.

---

## 4.

Risk management is an essential practice for maintaining a strong cybersecurity posture. By identifying and assessing risks, implementing mitigation strategies, and prioritizing efforts based on potential impact, organizations can reduce the likelihood of cyberattacks and protect their critical assets. Regularly revisiting and updating the risk management process is necessary to keep up with evolving threats in the dynamic cybersecurity landscape.

Effective risk management ensures that an organization can not only prevent attacks but also recover quickly when breaches occur, minimizing the overall impact on business operations.

# Chapter 7: Cybersecurity Frameworks

*Overview*

Cybersecurity frameworks provide structured guidelines, best practices, and standards that organizations can follow to secure their networks, data, and systems. These frameworks help businesses identify, manage, and mitigate cybersecurity risks while ensuring compliance with relevant laws and regulations. This chapter explores some of the most widely adopted cybersecurity frameworks, including NIST, ISO/IEC 27001, and CIS, and explains how these frameworks help businesses build robust cybersecurity programs.

---

## 1. Overview of Popular Cybersecurity Frameworks

*1.1 NIST Cybersecurity Framework (NIST CSF)*

The **National Institute of Standards and Technology (NIST)** Cybersecurity Framework is a set of guidelines developed to help organizations understand and manage cybersecurity risks. Originally created for critical infrastructure sectors in the U.S., it has since been widely adopted by organizations of all sizes and industries around the world.

**Key Components of NIST CSF:** The NIST CSF is organized into five core functions, each representing a critical area of cybersecurity management:

1. **Identify** - Develop an understanding of the organization's cybersecurity risks to systems, people, assets, data, and capabilities.
2. **Protect** - Implement safeguards to limit or contain the impact of potential cybersecurity events.
3. **Detect** - Implement activities to identify the occurrence of cybersecurity events in a timely manner.
4. **Respond** - Develop and implement appropriate activities to take action regarding a detected cybersecurity event.
5. **Recover** - Implement plans to restore any capabilities or services impaired during a cybersecurity event.

**How NIST CSF Helps Businesses:**

- **Risk Management:** NIST CSF provides a flexible framework for organizations to identify, assess, and manage risks based on their business context, risk tolerance, and resources.
- **Scalability:** The framework is adaptable and can be scaled to fit organizations of different sizes and sectors.

- **Improvement Cycle:** NIST encourages continuous improvement through monitoring and adjusting cybersecurity practices.

## *1.2 ISO/IEC 27001*

The **ISO/IEC 27001** standard is part of the larger ISO/IEC 27000 family of standards that focuses on information security management. ISO/IEC 27001 provides a systematic approach to managing sensitive company information, ensuring that it remains secure from threats such as data breaches, theft, and unauthorized access.

**Key Components of ISO/IEC 27001:**

- **Information Security Management System (ISMS):** The standard requires organizations to establish, implement, maintain, and continually improve an ISMS.
- **Risk Assessment and Treatment:** ISO/IEC 27001 requires organizations to identify and assess cybersecurity risks and implement appropriate measures to mitigate them.
- **Control Objectives and Controls:** The framework provides specific security controls that organizations can implement, including physical security, access control, incident management, and business continuity.

**How ISO/IEC 27001 Helps Businesses:**

- **Formalized Security Processes:** ISO/IEC 27001 helps businesses formalize their approach to cybersecurity by setting up an ISMS that integrates risk management, policies, and procedures.

- **Global Recognition:** Achieving ISO/IEC 27001 certification provides global recognition that a business has met a recognized standard of information security.

- **Continuous Improvement:** The standard emphasizes a continuous improvement model, ensuring that organizations constantly update their cybersecurity measures to adapt to evolving threats.

## *1.3 Center for Internet Security (CIS) Controls*

The **Center for Internet Security (CIS)** provides a set of best practices known as the **CIS Controls** (formerly known as the Critical Security Controls). The CIS Controls are designed to help organizations defend against the most common and impactful cybersecurity threats. These controls are a prioritized and actionable set of security practices.

**Key Components of CIS Controls:** The CIS Controls are made up of 18 high-level security controls that are further broken down into sub-controls. Some of the key controls include:

1. **Inventory of Authorized and Unauthorized Devices:** Maintaining an up-to-date inventory of all devices connected

to the network and ensuring that only authorized devices have access.

2. **Secure Configurations for Hardware and Software:** Implementing secure configurations for devices and software to minimize vulnerabilities.

3. **Continuous Vulnerability Management:** Continuously scanning for vulnerabilities and applying patches in a timely manner.

4. **Controlled Use of Administrative Privileges:** Limiting and monitoring the use of administrative privileges to reduce the risk of unauthorized access.

5. **Incident Response and Management:** Developing and implementing an incident response plan to quickly address any cybersecurity events.

**How CIS Controls Help Businesses:**

- **Practical and Actionable:** The CIS Controls provide businesses with practical steps they can take to reduce cybersecurity risks immediately.

- **Prioritized Approach:** The 18 controls are prioritized, helping organizations focus on the most critical security measures first.

- **Ease of Implementation:** The controls are designed to be straightforward and easy to implement, making them accessible to businesses of all sizes.

## 2. How Frameworks Help Businesses Structure Their Cybersecurity Efforts

Cybersecurity frameworks play a crucial role in guiding organizations to develop comprehensive, scalable, and effective cybersecurity programs. Here's how they can help businesses structure their cybersecurity efforts:

### *2.1 Establishing a Risk-Based Approach*

- Frameworks like **NIST CSF** and **ISO/IEC 27001** help businesses adopt a risk-based approach to cybersecurity. By focusing on identifying and managing risks, these frameworks guide organizations in prioritizing their resources on the most critical threats, rather than attempting to address every possible risk. This approach helps ensure that cybersecurity efforts are focused where they matter most.

### *2.2 Creating a Structured Security Plan*

- Cybersecurity frameworks provide businesses with a clear roadmap for developing a structured security plan. This plan typically includes:
  - Defining roles and responsibilities.
  - Identifying critical assets and data.

- o   Implementing security controls.
- o   Conducting regular security assessments.
- o   Establishing incident response protocols.

## *2.3 Compliance and Legal Requirements*

- Many organizations are required by law or industry regulations to comply with cybersecurity standards. Frameworks such as **ISO/IEC 27001** and **NIST CSF** help businesses meet these compliance requirements by providing guidelines for securing sensitive data and maintaining operational security. Achieving certification in these frameworks can also help businesses avoid regulatory fines and penalties.

## *2.4 Measuring Cybersecurity Effectiveness*

- Frameworks offer businesses a way to measure the effectiveness of their cybersecurity efforts. The **CIS Controls** provide a measurable set of security practices that can be assessed regularly to ensure that security controls are working as intended. By following these frameworks, organizations can track their progress in improving security posture over time.

## *2.5 Continuous Improvement*

- A key principle of cybersecurity frameworks is continuous improvement. Both **NIST CSF** and **ISO/IEC 27001** emphasize the need for ongoing evaluation and improvement of cybersecurity practices. By regularly revisiting and updating their cybersecurity strategies, organizations can ensure that they are always prepared for emerging threats and vulnerabilities.

## *2.6 Enhancing Organizational Security Culture*

- Frameworks like **ISO/IEC 27001** and **CIS Controls** stress the importance of employee training and awareness in maintaining a strong cybersecurity culture. By adopting a framework, businesses can implement formalized training programs and encourage a culture of security within the organization. This reduces the likelihood of human error, which is often a significant cause of data breaches.

## 3. Choosing the Right Framework for Your Business

The choice of cybersecurity framework largely depends on the business's needs, resources, and industry requirements. Here are some factors to consider when selecting a framework:

1. **Regulatory Requirements:**

o   Businesses in highly regulated industries (e.g., healthcare, finance) may need to adhere to specific frameworks like **HIPAA** (Health Insurance Portability and Accountability Act) or **NIST CSF** to comply with industry standards.

2. **Business Size and Complexity:**

o   Smaller businesses may find the **CIS Controls** more manageable due to its practical and prioritized approach, while larger organizations with more complex needs may benefit from the comprehensive **ISO/IEC 27001** or **NIST CSF** frameworks.

3. **Geographic Reach:**

o   For businesses operating internationally, the **GDPR** compliance requirements may make the **ISO/IEC 27001** framework a good fit, as it aligns with many global data protection regulations.

4. **Resources and Expertise:**

o   If the business lacks the in-house expertise to implement a complex framework like **ISO/IEC 27001**, starting with a more straightforward framework like **CIS Controls** can help get started with basic cybersecurity hygiene.

Cybersecurity frameworks are invaluable tools that help businesses structure their cybersecurity programs and ensure they meet best practices and compliance requirements. Whether it's the risk-based approach of **NIST CSF**, the systematic structure of **ISO/IEC 27001**, or the practical and prioritized guidelines of **CIS Controls**, these frameworks provide organizations with the tools they need to protect their critical assets and improve their overall security posture. By adopting and continuously refining these frameworks, businesses can better defend against the ever-evolving cyber threats in the digital age.

# Chapter 8: Securing Personal Devices: Computers, Phones, and Tablets

*Overview*

In today's digital world, personal devices such as computers, smartphones, and tablets store sensitive information, including personal data, financial details, and communication. These devices are often targets for cybercriminals seeking to steal information, compromise privacy, or gain unauthorized access to accounts. As such, securing personal devices is crucial for protecting yourself against a wide range of cyber threats. This chapter covers the best practices for securing personal devices and offers tips on device encryption, strong passwords, and two-factor authentication (2FA).

## 1. Best Practices for Securing Personal Devices

### 1.1 Keep Software Up to Date

One of the most important steps in securing personal devices is ensuring that all software is up to date. Regular updates often contain security patches that fix known vulnerabilities, making it harder for hackers to exploit your devices.

- **Operating System Updates:** Ensure that your computer, phone, and tablet are always running the latest version of the operating system. This applies to both desktop and mobile devices (Windows, macOS, iOS, Android).

- **Example:** Enable automatic updates on your devices so that you don't miss out on essential security patches.

- **Application and Software Updates:** In addition to the operating system, update applications such as browsers, email clients, and third-party apps. Many apps have vulnerabilities that hackers can exploit if they are not updated regularly.

- **Example:** Regularly update apps like Google Chrome, Microsoft Office, or Adobe Acrobat Reader to close any security holes.

### 1.2 Install Antivirus and Anti-malware Software

Protect your devices from malicious software (malware) by installing reputable antivirus and anti-malware software. These programs help detect, quarantine, and remove threats before they can cause harm.

- **Desktop Devices:** For Windows and macOS computers, reliable antivirus software like Norton, Bitdefender, or McAfee can offer protection from a wide range of threats, including viruses, ransomware, and spyware.
- **Mobile Devices:** While smartphones and tablets are generally less vulnerable to malware, it's still a good practice

to install mobile security apps like Avast Mobile Security or Lookout for Android and iOS.

### 1.3 Enable Firewalls

A firewall is a security system that monitors and controls incoming and outgoing network traffic based on predetermined security rules. Enabling a firewall on your devices helps prevent unauthorized access to your device from external sources.

- **Computer Firewalls:** Both Windows and macOS have built-in firewalls. Ensure they are activated to provide an extra layer of protection.
- **Mobile Devices:** Although mobile operating systems typically have firewall protections, third-party apps like NetGuard (for Android) or using a VPN (Virtual Private Network) can enhance security.

### 1.4 Secure Wi-Fi Networks

Ensure that your Wi-Fi network is secured using strong encryption and a strong password. Avoid using public Wi-Fi for sensitive activities like online banking or shopping.

- **Wi-Fi Encryption:** Use WPA3 encryption (or at least WPA2) for your home Wi-Fi network. Disable WEP encryption, as it is outdated and easily cracked.

- **VPN (Virtual Private Network):** When accessing public Wi-Fi, use a VPN to encrypt your internet connection and prevent attackers from intercepting your data.

---

## 2. Device Encryption: Protecting Your Data

### 2.1 What is Device Encryption?

Device encryption is the process of converting the data stored on your device into a format that cannot be read without proper decryption keys. This ensures that even if someone gains access to your device, they cannot access your personal information.

- **Full Disk Encryption (FDE):** FDE encrypts the entire device, including the operating system, applications, and data. Both macOS and Windows have built-in FDE tools: **FileVault** for macOS and **BitLocker** for Windows.
- **Mobile Device Encryption:** Both Android and iOS devices come with built-in encryption tools that automatically encrypt data when the device is locked with a passcode. Ensure that your device is encrypted by enabling a strong password or PIN.

### 2.2 How to Enable Encryption on Personal Devices:

- **On Windows (BitLocker):**

- o Go to **Control Panel → System and Security → BitLocker Drive Encryption**.
- o Choose the drive to encrypt, and follow the prompts to set up BitLocker encryption.
- **On macOS (FileVault):**
  - o Go to **System Preferences → Security & Privacy → FileVault**.
  - o Click the lock to make changes and turn on FileVault.
- **On Android:**
  - o On newer Android devices, encryption is enabled by default when you set a PIN or password. To verify, go to **Settings → Security → Encryption**.
- **On iOS:**
  - o iPhones and iPads automatically encrypt data when a passcode is set. To ensure encryption, go to **Settings → Face ID & Passcode** (or **Touch ID & Passcode**), and enable a strong passcode.

## *2.3 Benefits of Device Encryption:*

- **Protects Data in Case of Loss or Theft:** If your device is lost or stolen, encrypted data cannot be accessed without the decryption key or passcode.
- **Compliance with Privacy Laws:** Encryption is often a legal requirement for protecting sensitive data, especially in industries like healthcare and finance.

# 3. Strong Passwords: Creating and Managing Secure Access

## 3.1 Why Strong Passwords Matter

Passwords are often the first line of defense in protecting your devices and online accounts. Weak passwords can be easily guessed or cracked, leaving your personal information vulnerable to theft.

## 3.2 Tips for Creating Strong Passwords:

- **Length:** A strong password should be at least 12 characters long.
- **Complexity:** Use a mix of uppercase and lowercase letters, numbers, and special characters (e.g., @, #, $).
- **Avoid Common Words:** Avoid using easily guessable information, such as names, birthdates, or common words like "password."
- **Use Passphrases:** A passphrase, such as "Blue$Sky2023!," can be both secure and easier to remember.

## 3.3 Password Management:

- **Password Managers:** Use a password manager like LastPass, 1Password, or Bitwarden to securely store and generate complex passwords. Password managers can create unique, strong passwords for each of your accounts and allow you to access them with a master password.

- **Avoid Reusing Passwords:** Reusing the same password across multiple accounts increases the risk of a breach. A password manager can help you avoid this.

## 4. Two-Factor Authentication (2FA): Adding an Extra Layer of Protection

### 4.1 What is Two-Factor Authentication (2FA)?

Two-factor authentication (2FA) is an additional security layer that requires users to provide two forms of identification before accessing an account or device. The two factors typically involve something you know (your password) and something you have (e.g., a smartphone or security token).

### 4.2 How 2FA Works:

1. **Something You Know:** Your password or PIN.
2. **Something You Have:** A physical device like your smartphone, where you receive a one-time code (OTP), or a hardware token (e.g., YubiKey).
3. **Something You Are:** Biometric authentication (e.g., fingerprint, face recognition) is also increasingly used as a factor.

## *4.3 Enabling 2FA:*

- **On Google Accounts:** Go to **Security** → **2-Step Verification** and follow the instructions to set up 2FA using Google Authenticator or an SMS code.
- **On Facebook:** Go to **Settings** → **Security and Login** → **Use two-factor authentication** and choose your preferred method of authentication (e.g., Authenticator app, SMS).
- **On Smartphones:** Many mobile apps (banking, email, etc.) support 2FA. Ensure it's enabled in the app's security settings to add an extra layer of protection.

## *4.4 Benefits of 2FA:*

- **Enhanced Security:** Even if an attacker gains access to your password, they cannot log in without the second form of authentication.
- **Protection Against Phishing:** 2FA provides an extra barrier against phishing attacks, where attackers may trick users into revealing their passwords.

---

## 5.

Securing personal devices is crucial in protecting sensitive information and ensuring privacy in today's connected world. By implementing best practices such as regular software updates, device encryption, using strong passwords, and enabling two-factor authentication (2FA), individuals can significantly reduce the risk of cyberattacks and data theft. The combination of these measures forms a strong defense against the most common cyber threats, safeguarding your personal data and digital privacy from potential breaches and unauthorized access.

# Chapter 9: Firewalls and Antivirus Software

*Overview*

Firewalls and antivirus software are two of the most fundamental tools in any cybersecurity strategy. They play a crucial role in defending against both external and internal threats by controlling the flow of data and detecting malicious activities. This chapter explains how firewalls and antivirus software work, their importance in protecting against cyber threats, and recommends solutions for different platforms.

## 1. How Firewalls Protect Against External and Internal Threats

A **firewall** is a network security system that monitors and controls incoming and outgoing network traffic based on predetermined security rules. Firewalls are designed to protect a computer or network from unauthorized access, attacks, or other harmful activities. They serve as the first line of defense against external cyber threats, such as hackers or malicious software.

*Key Functions of a Firewall:*

1. **Network Traffic Filtering:**

- o Firewalls analyze incoming and outgoing traffic to determine whether it should be allowed or blocked. Traffic is filtered based on various parameters, including IP addresses, ports, protocols, and content.
- o **Example:** A firewall may block all incoming traffic from an untrusted IP address or limit access to certain ports (such as ports used for remote desktop or file-sharing services) to prevent unauthorized access.

2. **Blocking Malicious Activities:**
   - o Firewalls can identify known malicious signatures (patterns of behavior) and block them before they can affect the network.
   - o **Example:** If a firewall detects that an incoming request is part of a Distributed Denial of Service (DDoS) attack, it can block the traffic to protect the network.

3. **Internal Threat Protection:**
   - o While firewalls primarily protect against external threats, they can also help mitigate internal risks by preventing unauthorized communication between devices within the same network.
   - o **Example:** If an employee's device is infected with malware, the firewall can restrict the device from communicating with other parts of the internal network, thus containing the infection.

4. **VPN Support:**

   o Many firewalls support Virtual Private Networks (VPNs), which create secure tunnels for remote workers to connect to the organization's network safely.

   o **Example:** A remote worker can securely connect to the company's internal network through an encrypted VPN, ensuring that no malicious actors can intercept their traffic.

## *Types of Firewalls:*

1. **Packet-Filtering Firewalls:**

   o The simplest type of firewall, which checks each packet of data sent across the network and allows or blocks it based on predefined rules.

   o **Limitations:** Does not inspect the content of the data packets, which can make it less effective against sophisticated attacks.

2. **Stateful Inspection Firewalls:**

   o These firewalls track the state of active connections and make decisions based on the state of the traffic (e.g., whether a connection is established or part of an existing session).

- o **Advantages:** Provides more security than packet-filtering firewalls by examining the entire session rather than just individual packets.

3. **Next-Generation Firewalls (NGFW):**
   - o NGFWs combine the features of traditional firewalls with additional capabilities, such as application awareness, intrusion prevention systems (IPS), and deep packet inspection (DPI).
   - o **Advantages:** They offer comprehensive protection by detecting and blocking sophisticated threats, such as application-layer attacks.

# 2. How Antivirus Software Protects Against External and Internal Threats

**Antivirus software** is a type of program designed to detect, prevent, and remove malicious software (malware) from a computer or network. Malware includes viruses, worms, Trojans, ransomware, spyware, and more. Antivirus software provides protection by scanning files, programs, and applications for known patterns or suspicious behavior that may indicate the presence of malware.

*Key Functions of Antivirus Software:*

1. **Malware Detection:**

- o Antivirus software uses signature-based detection to identify known malware by comparing files on your system to a database of known malware signatures.
- o **Example:** If a user downloads an email attachment that contains a virus, the antivirus software will recognize the signature of the virus and prevent it from executing.

2. **Real-Time Scanning:**
   - o Antivirus software scans files, programs, and websites in real time as you interact with them. This prevents malware from being executed or installed on your system in the first place.
   - o **Example:** When you download a file from the internet, the antivirus scans it immediately before allowing you to open or execute it.

3. **Heuristic Analysis:**
   - o Modern antivirus software uses heuristic analysis to identify unknown threats by analyzing the behavior of suspicious files or programs. If a program behaves like malware, the software will flag it as potentially harmful.
   - o **Example:** If a program attempts to modify system files or encrypt data without the user's knowledge (a typical behavior of ransomware), the antivirus will block the action.

4. **Quarantine and Removal:**
    o When a potential threat is detected, antivirus software isolates it in a quarantine folder to prevent it from causing harm. The user is then notified and given the option to remove or repair the infected file.
    o **Example:** If the antivirus detects a Trojan in a downloaded file, it will move the file to quarantine, preventing the Trojan from running until the user decides what to do.

5. **Protection Against Phishing:**
    o Antivirus software often includes features that detect phishing attempts, such as fraudulent websites or emails designed to steal login credentials or personal information.
    o **Example:** If you receive an email with a link that leads to a fake bank website, the antivirus may alert you that the site is malicious and block access to it.

*Types of Antivirus Software:*

1. **Signature-Based Antivirus:**
    o Detects malware by comparing the files on the system to a database of known virus signatures. This method is effective against known threats but can miss new or modified malware.

- ○ **Example:** Norton Antivirus uses signature-based detection to recognize and block known viruses.

2. **Heuristic Antivirus:**

   - ○ Uses heuristic analysis to identify unknown threats based on behavior and patterns. This method can catch new and emerging malware but may result in false positives.

   - ○ **Example:** Bitdefender uses heuristic scanning to detect zero-day threats (new malware not yet identified in the signature database).

3. **Cloud-Based Antivirus:**

   - ○ Runs antivirus scans in the cloud rather than on the device itself. This reduces the system's resource usage and allows for faster updates and more accurate threat detection.

   - ○ **Example:** Panda Security offers cloud-based antivirus protection that leverages cloud computing to detect threats in real time.

---

# 3. Recommended Firewall and Antivirus Solutions for Different Platforms

## 3.1 Firewalls for Different Platforms:

1. **Windows:**

    o **Windows Defender Firewall** (built-in): A free and effective firewall that is integrated into the Windows operating system. It provides basic protection and can be customized with rules for incoming and outgoing traffic.

    o **ZoneAlarm** (third-party): A popular third-party firewall for Windows that provides advanced protection features, including real-time monitoring, identity protection, and anti-phishing.

2. **macOS:**

    o **macOS Firewall** (built-in): The default firewall on macOS, offering basic protection against unauthorized network access. It is easy to enable through the System Preferences menu.

    o **Little Snitch** (third-party): A more advanced firewall solution for macOS that provides detailed control over network traffic, alerting users to suspicious or outgoing connections.

3. **Linux:**

    o **UFW (Uncomplicated Firewall)**: A simple and user-friendly firewall for Linux, often used for server protection. It is great for managing network traffic and providing basic security.

- o **iptables**: A more advanced firewall tool used to filter traffic and set up complex rules on Linux-based systems.

4. **Mobile Devices (iOS/Android):**
   - o While mobile operating systems (iOS/Android) come with built-in firewall protections, apps like **NetGuard** (Android) provide additional control over mobile network connections, helping to block malicious or suspicious traffic.

## *3.2 Antivirus Software for Different Platforms:*

1. **Windows:**
   - o **Norton 360:** A comprehensive antivirus solution with real-time protection, cloud backup, and VPN services. Ideal for protecting Windows devices from a wide range of threats.
   - o **Bitdefender Antivirus Plus:** A powerful antivirus program for Windows that offers real-time protection, ransomware protection, and anti-phishing features.

2. **macOS:**
   - o **Intego Mac Internet Security X9:** A well-regarded antivirus for macOS, offering real-time protection against malware, phishing attacks, and more.

- ○ **Sophos Home:** A reliable antivirus for macOS with real-time protection, web filtering, and ransomware protection.

3. **Android:**
   - ○ **Avast Mobile Security:** A comprehensive mobile antivirus solution that protects against malware, phishing, and theft. It also includes anti-theft tools, privacy features, and app lock functionality.
   - ○ **Kaspersky Mobile Antivirus:** A highly rated mobile security app that offers protection from malware, theft, and privacy breaches on Android devices.

4. **iOS:**
   - ○ **Lookout Mobile Security:** Although iOS is generally less susceptible to malware, Lookout provides additional features such as theft protection, data breach alerts, and secure Wi-Fi connection monitoring.
   - ○ **McAfee Mobile Security:** Provides a range of features, including anti-theft, app privacy checks, and safe web browsing for iOS devices.

**4.**

Firewalls and antivirus software are essential tools for protecting personal devices from a wide range of cyber threats. By blocking unauthorized access and preventing malware infections, these tools serve as a crucial first line of defense for individuals and businesses alike. Implementing the right firewall and antivirus solutions, tailored to the specific platform, helps ensure that your devices remain secure and that sensitive information stays protected. Regular updates, effective configuration, and supplementary security practices (such as using a VPN) further enhance the security of personal devices.

# Chapter 10: Securing IoT Devices

## *Overview*

The **Internet of Things (IoT)** refers to a network of interconnected devices, sensors, and smart objects that communicate with each other and with centralized systems over the internet. These devices, ranging from smart thermostats and wearables to home security cameras and industrial machines, are transforming the way we live and work. However, IoT devices can present significant security risks due to their widespread adoption and often insufficient security measures. This chapter explores the risks associated with IoT devices and provides practical advice on how to secure them and avoid common vulnerabilities.

---

## 1. Risks Associated with Internet of Things (IoT) Devices

### *1.1 Lack of Security by Design*

Many IoT devices are manufactured with little regard for security, prioritizing ease of use, affordability, and functionality over strong cybersecurity measures. As a result, these devices may have weak or non-existent security features, making them vulnerable to exploitation.

- **Default Passwords and Weak Authentication:** Many IoT devices come with default usernames and passwords, which are often easy for attackers to guess. If users fail to change these defaults, it opens the door to unauthorized access.

- ○ **Example:** A popular smart camera company shipped devices with the default password "admin," which many users failed to change. Hackers exploited this vulnerability to gain unauthorized access to thousands of devices.

## *1.2 Insecure Communication*

Many IoT devices transmit data over networks without proper encryption, exposing sensitive information to potential eavesdropping and interception by attackers.

- **Unencrypted Traffic:** Data sent by IoT devices may not be encrypted, allowing attackers to intercept it during transmission.
  - ○ **Example:** A smart home system that transmits unencrypted data can expose personal information like daily routines or access codes to malicious actors.
- **Lack of Secure Protocols:** IoT devices may use insecure communication protocols such as HTTP instead of HTTPS, making it easier for attackers to manipulate or hijack communications.

## *1.3 Insufficient Updates and Patching*

Many IoT devices lack proper update mechanisms or rely on outdated firmware that is no longer supported by the manufacturer. This makes it difficult to address known vulnerabilities in the device, leaving it open to attacks.

- **Outdated Firmware and Software:** As IoT devices age, manufacturers may stop providing updates, leaving security gaps. Attackers can exploit these vulnerabilities in older devices.
    - o **Example:** A large-scale botnet attack, known as **Mirai**, exploited IoT devices running outdated firmware to create a massive network of compromised devices for launching Distributed Denial of Service (DDoS) attacks.

*1.4 Physical Security Risks*

Many IoT devices are deployed in unsecured locations or are physically accessible to unauthorized individuals. An attacker can gain access to a device and tamper with it, compromising its integrity and security.

- **Physical Tampering:** Attackers may steal or physically manipulate IoT devices to gain access to the data or alter their functionality.

- o **Example:** A hacker with physical access to an unsecured smart lock system can attempt to bypass its security and gain entry to a home or office.

### *1.5 Privacy Risks*

IoT devices often collect personal and sensitive data, such as health information, location data, and household patterns. If these devices are not adequately protected, they can become a goldmine for attackers looking to exploit private information.

- **Data Collection and Sharing:** Many IoT devices continuously collect data, and without proper security, this data could be accessed or shared with unauthorized parties.
  - o **Example:** Smart speakers, such as Amazon Alexa or Google Home, could record conversations without the user's knowledge or consent, posing a privacy risk.

## 2. How to Secure Smart Devices and Avoid Common Vulnerabilities

### *2.1 Change Default Passwords*

One of the most critical steps in securing IoT devices is changing the default passwords that come with them. Manufacturers often provide generic credentials that are widely known and easy to exploit. Always set strong, unique passwords for each device.

- **Best Practices:**
  - Use long, complex passwords with a combination of letters, numbers, and special characters.
  - Avoid using easily guessable information such as your name, birthdate, or common words.
  - Use a password manager to store and generate strong passwords for multiple IoT devices.

## *2.2 Enable Two-Factor Authentication (2FA)*

Whenever possible, enable two-factor authentication (2FA) for IoT devices. 2FA provides an extra layer of protection by requiring a second form of verification, such as a code sent to your mobile phone or generated by an authenticator app.

- **Example:** If your smart home system supports 2FA, enable it so that even if someone steals your password, they still need access to your second authentication factor to compromise your device.

## *2.3 Secure Network Connections*

Ensure that IoT devices use encrypted communication to protect data from being intercepted by attackers. Always prefer IoT devices that support secure communication protocols such as HTTPS or encrypted Wi-Fi (WPA2 or WPA3).

- **Secure Wi-Fi:** Make sure your home or office Wi-Fi network is protected with WPA2 or WPA3 encryption and a strong password.

- **VPN for IoT Devices:** If possible, use a VPN to encrypt traffic between IoT devices and the internet. This helps to prevent man-in-the-middle attacks and ensures secure data transfer.

  o **Example:** If you have a smart thermostat, consider setting up a VPN or using an IoT-specific security appliance to ensure the device's traffic is encrypted and protected.

### 2.4 Regularly Update Device Firmware

Manufacturers regularly release firmware updates to patch vulnerabilities, fix bugs, and enhance the security of IoT devices. It's essential to keep devices up to date to ensure that they remain protected against newly discovered threats.

- **How to Keep Devices Updated:**
  o Enable automatic updates on devices that support it.
  o Periodically check the manufacturer's website for updates and install them promptly.
  o Set a reminder to check for updates on devices that do not support automatic updates.

### 2.5 Isolate IoT Devices on a Separate Network

To reduce the risk of IoT devices being compromised and accessing sensitive information on your primary network, isolate them on a separate network. Many modern routers offer a "guest network" or the ability to create isolated subnets for IoT devices.

- **Benefits of Isolation:**
  - Prevents compromised devices from accessing sensitive information such as passwords, banking data, or work-related documents.
  - Limits the damage in case one device is breached.
  - **Example:** Set up a separate Wi-Fi network for your smart home devices, ensuring they don't have direct access to your main network where you store sensitive information.

### *2.6 Disable Unnecessary Features*

Many IoT devices come with features that may not be necessary for your use, such as remote access, voice control, or automatic updates. Disabling these features when not in use reduces the potential attack surface.

- **Examples:**
  - Turn off remote access features if you don't need them.
  - Disable any voice or audio recording features when not in use to protect your privacy.

    o   If your device has a camera, ensure that it can only be activated when necessary.

### 2.7 Monitor Device Activity

Regularly monitor the activity and behavior of your IoT devices to detect any unusual or suspicious activity. Many devices provide logs or alerts that can notify you of potential security issues or unauthorized access attempts.

- **Examples of Monitoring:**
  - o Use a network monitoring tool to track IoT device activity and ensure no unusual behavior is occurring (e.g., large data transfers, device reboots).
  - o Set up notifications for unauthorized logins or configuration changes.

### 2.8 Physical Security

In addition to securing your device's digital defenses, ensure that it is physically secure. If the device is in a vulnerable location, consider moving it to a more secure area or locking it in a protected space.

- **Example:** A smart camera should be placed in a location that is difficult to tamper with. Use tamper-proof screws or enclosures to prevent physical access to the device.

**3.**

Securing IoT devices is critical in today's interconnected world, where vulnerabilities in everyday objects can lead to significant privacy and security breaches. By following best practices such as changing default passwords, enabling encryption, isolating devices on separate networks, and regularly updating firmware, users can reduce the risk of their IoT devices being compromised. As the number of connected devices continues to grow, implementing these security measures is essential for maintaining privacy, ensuring safe operation, and protecting against potential cyberattacks.

# Chapter 11: Understanding Network Security

*Overview*

Network security refers to the measures and protocols implemented to protect the integrity, confidentiality, and availability of data and systems connected to a network. As organizations increasingly rely on interconnected systems for operations, the need for robust network security has never been more critical. Cyberattacks, unauthorized access, and data breaches can cripple an organization, cause financial loss, and damage its reputation. This chapter provides an in-depth look at what network security is, why it's critical for organizations, and the essential components of network security, such as firewalls, intrusion detection systems (IDS), and virtual private networks (VPNs).

---

## 1. What is Network Security and Why It's Critical for Organizations

Network security is a set of technologies, processes, and practices designed to safeguard the integrity and confidentiality of an organization's data and networks from threats, such as cyberattacks, data breaches, and other unauthorized access or disruptions. Network security ensures that only authorized users, devices, and applications can access or communicate over a network, thus minimizing the risks associated with data loss, theft, or alteration.

*Key Reasons Why Network Security is Critical:*

1. **Protection Against Cyberattacks:**
   - Cyberattacks such as Distributed Denial of Service (DDoS), ransomware, and phishing are constantly evolving. A solid network security infrastructure helps protect the organization from these threats, ensuring that sensitive data is safe from malicious actors.

2. **Data Protection and Privacy:**
   - Organizations store vast amounts of personal, financial, and intellectual property data that need to be protected from unauthorized access. Network security ensures that data remains confidential and is only accessible to authorized users and devices.

3. **Business Continuity:**
   - Without proper network security, an organization could suffer from prolonged downtime due to system breaches, potentially resulting in significant financial losses. Effective network security minimizes downtime by preventing attacks that could disrupt services.

4. **Compliance with Regulatory Standards:**

o Many industries, such as healthcare, finance, and government, are governed by strict data protection regulations (e.g., GDPR, HIPAA). Network security is crucial for meeting compliance standards and avoiding fines or legal penalties.

5. **Protection Against Internal Threats:**

   o While external cybercriminals pose significant risks, internal threats (e.g., employees, contractors) can also jeopardize an organization's network security. Strong network security measures help detect and prevent malicious activities from insiders.

# 2. Components of Network Security

Network security involves multiple layers of defense to protect data, users, and systems from both external and internal threats. Below are some of the most common components of a comprehensive network security strategy:

## 2.1 Firewalls

A **firewall** is a network security system that monitors and controls incoming and outgoing network traffic based on predetermined security rules. It serves as a barrier between a trusted internal network and untrusted external networks, such as the internet.

- **Function of a Firewall:**
  - Firewalls filter network traffic based on specific rules to allow legitimate traffic and block malicious or unauthorized access. They can be configured to block or permit traffic based on IP addresses, ports, and protocols.
- **Types of Firewalls:**

0.  **Packet-Filtering Firewalls:** The simplest type of firewall, which inspects packets of data (units of communication transmitted over a network) and allows or blocks them based on predefined rules.

  - **Example:** Blocking access to a certain IP address or port (e.g., blocking external access to the company's internal server).
  1. **Stateful Inspection Firewalls:** More advanced than packet-filtering, these firewalls monitor the state of active connections and decide whether incoming packets are part of an established connection.
  2. **Next-Generation Firewalls (NGFWs):** These firewalls offer deeper inspection capabilities, including application awareness, intrusion prevention systems (IPS), and advanced threat detection, providing a higher level of security.
- **Benefits of Firewalls:**

o   Prevent unauthorized access to internal systems and resources.

o   Block malicious traffic (e.g., hackers, malware).

o   Enforce security policies and restrictions (e.g., prevent access to specific websites or ports).

## *2.2 Intrusion Detection Systems (IDS)*

An **Intrusion Detection System (IDS)** is a device or software application that monitors network traffic for suspicious activity or violations of security policies. IDS systems help detect unauthorized access or anomalous behavior within a network and alert administrators so that they can take appropriate action.

- **How IDS Works:**
    - o   IDS works by monitoring network traffic or system behavior and comparing it to a database of known attack patterns or anomalies. When a potential threat is detected, the system triggers an alert.
    - o   **Example:** If an employee's account attempts to access sensitive files at unusual hours, an IDS would flag this as suspicious activity.
- **Types of IDS:**

0.   **Network-based IDS (NIDS):** Monitors traffic flowing through the network and analyzes packets for potential threats. NIDS is typically deployed at network entry points (e.g., routers).

1. **Host-based IDS (HIDS):** Monitors the activities of individual hosts (e.g., servers or workstations) and looks for suspicious behavior, such as unauthorized file modifications.

- **IDS vs. IPS:**

  o **IDS** only detects and alerts on suspicious activity, while **Intrusion Prevention Systems (IPS)** not only detects but also actively blocks threats in real time.

- **Benefits of IDS:**
  o Helps detect cyberattacks early, reducing the potential damage.
  o Provides insight into network traffic, helping administrators identify vulnerabilities.
  o Improves incident response by providing alerts and context around potential attacks.

## *2.3 Virtual Private Networks (VPNs)*

A **Virtual Private Network (VPN)** is a tool that allows users to securely connect to a network over the internet, encrypting the data traffic between the user and the network. VPNs provide a secure and private communication channel, even over untrusted networks like public Wi-Fi.

- **How VPNs Work:**

o VPNs create an encrypted "tunnel" between the user's device and the network. This tunnel ensures that even if the data is intercepted, it cannot be read without the decryption key.

o **Example:** When employees connect remotely to a company's internal network, they use a VPN to ensure their internet traffic is encrypted, preventing attackers from eavesdropping.

- **Types of VPNs:**

0.  **Remote Access VPN:** Used by individual users to connect securely to a private network from a remote location.

   1.  **Site-to-Site VPN:** Used to connect two or more networks securely over the internet, often used by businesses with multiple locations.

- **Benefits of VPNs:**

   o **Privacy and Anonymity:** VPNs hide a user's IP address and encrypt internet traffic, making it difficult for hackers or third parties to track online activities.

   o **Secure Remote Access:** VPNs allow employees to securely access corporate resources from any location, protecting data from being intercepted on public or unsecured networks.

- o **Bypassing Geographical Restrictions:** VPNs can help users bypass regional censorship or restrictions by routing traffic through servers in different locations.

## *2.4 Additional Network Security Tools*

1. **Network Access Control (NAC):** Ensures that only authorized devices can connect to the network by enforcing security policies such as checking whether devices have up-to-date antivirus software or the latest patches before they are granted access.

2. **Email Security:** Tools that scan emails for potential threats like phishing, malware, or attachments containing malicious content. Examples include email filters and anti-spam solutions.

3. **Sandboxing:** A security technique used to isolate potentially harmful software, allowing it to run in a controlled environment without affecting the main system.

# 3. How Network Security Protects Organizations

Network security provides multiple layers of protection for an organization's IT infrastructure and data. By implementing security solutions like firewalls, IDS, and VPNs, organizations can safeguard their networks from external and internal threats. Here's how network security components work together to protect business operations:

### 3.1 Defends Against External Attacks

Firewalls and IDS can block malicious traffic from the outside, preventing hackers, malware, and other threats from gaining unauthorized access to the network. Firewalls filter incoming and outgoing traffic, while IDS can detect and alert on suspicious activity that might signal an intrusion attempt.

### 3.2 Secures Remote Access

VPNs ensure that remote workers can access corporate resources securely, even when connected to public or unsecured networks. This prevents attackers from intercepting sensitive data, such as login credentials or confidential files, as they travel over the internet.

### 3.3 Detects and Responds to Anomalies

IDS tools help detect potential attacks early by monitoring network traffic and system behavior. By identifying anomalies or known attack patterns, IDS can alert administrators to take action before a breach occurs.

### 3.4 Protects Sensitive Data

Network security protocols such as encryption, access control, and VPNs ensure that sensitive data is protected both in transit and at rest, reducing the risk of data breaches and unauthorized access.

## 4.

Network security is an essential part of an organization's overall cybersecurity strategy. By implementing a combination of firewalls, intrusion detection systems, and virtual private networks, businesses can protect their networks from external and internal threats, safeguard sensitive data, and maintain business continuity. These network security components not only help prevent cyberattacks but also ensure compliance with industry regulations and standards, ultimately supporting a secure and resilient digital environment for the organization.

# Chapter 12: Building a Secure Network

## *Overview*

Building a secure network is one of the most fundamental aspects of safeguarding an organization's digital infrastructure. A properly designed and secured network ensures the confidentiality, integrity, and availability of data while minimizing the risk of unauthorized access, data breaches, and cyberattacks. This chapter will explore key strategies for building a secure network architecture and provide best practices for segmenting networks and securing communication channels to protect organizational assets.

---

## 1. Key Strategies for Building a Secure Network Architecture

### *1.1 Defense in Depth*

**Defense in Depth** is a security strategy that involves multiple layers of defense to protect a network from various threats. This approach recognizes that no single security measure is sufficient to stop all types of cyberattacks, and as such, it combines various tools, policies, and practices to mitigate risks at different points in the network.

- **Multiple Layers of Security:** Implementing a layered security model helps ensure that if one layer is breached, other defenses will still be in place to thwart the attack.
  - Example: Firewalls at the perimeter, intrusion detection systems (IDS) monitoring internal traffic, and endpoint security tools on devices all form part of a defense-in-depth strategy.

## 1.2 Network Redundancy and Fault Tolerance

To ensure that the network remains functional even in the event of hardware failure, cyberattacks, or other disruptions, **network redundancy** and **fault tolerance** are crucial.

- **Redundant Components:** Implementing redundant systems, including backup power supplies, network paths, and failover systems, ensures that there is no single point of failure.
  - Example: A company might have multiple internet service providers and routers configured in a way that if one connection fails, traffic will automatically be rerouted through another provider or router.
- **Load Balancing:** Distributing network traffic across multiple servers or connections helps prevent any single resource from being overwhelmed.
  - Example: During peak usage times, a website might use load balancing to distribute incoming requests

across multiple servers, maintaining availability and performance.

## 1.3 Implementing Strong Access Control

Restricting network access based on user roles and privileges is a fundamental security practice. **Role-based access control (RBAC)** ensures that users can only access the data and resources they need to perform their job functions.

- **Principle of Least Privilege (PoLP):** Users, devices, and applications should be granted the minimum access necessary to perform their tasks.
  - **Example:** A finance department employee should not have access to the company's HR database, and an HR employee should not have access to sensitive financial data.

## 1.4 Regular Network Monitoring and Logging

Continuous monitoring and logging are critical for detecting and responding to potential security incidents.

- **Network Traffic Analysis:** Monitoring network traffic for unusual patterns can help identify potential security breaches, such as large-scale data exfiltration or internal reconnaissance by an attacker.
- **Logging:** Log all network activity to provide a historical record that can be reviewed in case of an incident, helping to

identify how an attack occurred and how it can be prevented in the future.

### 1.5 Secure Remote Access

With the rise of remote work, ensuring that employees can securely access company resources from outside the office is essential.

- **VPN (Virtual Private Network):** A VPN provides a secure, encrypted connection between remote workers and the company's internal network, ensuring that data transmitted over public networks remains protected.
  - o **Example:** Employees working from home can securely access internal systems and resources by connecting to the company network via a VPN, preventing unauthorized access and data interception.

## 2. Best Practices for Segmenting Networks

Network segmentation involves dividing a network into multiple smaller, isolated segments to reduce the scope of potential damage in case of a breach and to control access to sensitive data.

### 2.1 Logical Segmentation with VLANs

**Virtual Local Area Networks (VLANs)** allow administrators to create logically segmented networks within the same physical network. This enables network isolation based on roles, departments, or security requirements, regardless of physical location.

- **VLANs for Isolation:** Sensitive departments or resources (e.g., finance, HR) can be placed on separate VLANs, restricting access to these resources from other departments.
  - o **Example:** The IT department may have access to administrative servers, while the marketing department only has access to public-facing systems. These two departments can be on different VLANs to isolate their traffic and reduce the risk of lateral movement by attackers.

## *2.2 Implementing Demilitarized Zones (DMZ)*

A **Demilitarized Zone (DMZ)** is a segment of the network that acts as a buffer zone between the internal network and the outside world. It is typically used to house publicly accessible services, such as web servers, email servers, and DNS servers.

- **Purpose of DMZ:** The DMZ is exposed to the internet, but access from the DMZ to the internal network is restricted, ensuring that external threats can be contained in the DMZ and preventing them from reaching critical internal systems.
  - o **Example:** A company's website and email servers are placed in the DMZ, but internal financial databases are inaccessible from the DMZ. This

isolation reduces the risk of an attack spreading from external services to internal systems.

## 2.3 Micro-Segmentation

**Micro-segmentation** takes network segmentation a step further by dividing the network into even smaller segments, often at the application level, allowing more granular control over who can access specific resources.

- **Segmentation at the Application Layer:** This involves segmenting traffic between specific applications or even between different components of a single application, ensuring that only authorized users and devices can interact with particular services.
  - o **Example:** In a cloud environment, micro-segmentation might separate services like databases, web servers, and application servers into isolated segments, limiting access to each based on strict security policies.

## 2.4 Zero Trust Architecture

The **Zero Trust** model operates on the assumption that no user, device, or application—whether inside or outside the organization's network—is inherently trustworthy. Instead, trust is continually verified based on the principle of least privilege, and access is granted only if the user or device meets specific security requirements.

- **Continuous Authentication and Authorization:** Zero Trust requires continuous verification of identity and context for every request, ensuring that only legitimate users and devices can access network resources.
  - o **Example:** Even after a user logs into a system, Zero Trust ensures that access is only granted based on specific attributes (e.g., IP address, device health, or behavior) and that access is revoked immediately when it is no longer required.

## 3. Best Practices for Securing Communication Channels

### *3.1 Encrypting Network Traffic*

**Encryption** is one of the most effective ways to secure communication channels and protect data during transmission. Encrypting network traffic ensures that even if data is intercepted, it cannot be read or tampered with.

- **Encryption Protocols:**
  - o **TLS (Transport Layer Security):** Use TLS to secure communication channels, such as HTTP over SSL (HTTPS), ensuring secure web traffic.

- o **VPN Encryption:** Ensure that remote communication is encrypted via VPNs, providing secure tunnels for data transmission.
- **End-to-End Encryption:** For particularly sensitive communications, implement end-to-end encryption, where data is encrypted at the source and decrypted only by the intended recipient.

### 3.2 Secure Wireless Networks

Wireless networks are particularly vulnerable to interception and unauthorized access if not secured properly. Implementing proper security measures on Wi-Fi networks is essential.

- **Use WPA3 Encryption:** Ensure that your Wi-Fi network uses the latest encryption standards, such as WPA3 (Wi-Fi Protected Access 3), to protect wireless traffic from eavesdropping.
- **Disable WPS:** Wi-Fi Protected Setup (WPS) is often vulnerable to brute-force attacks. It's recommended to disable this feature and rely on a strong WPA3 password.
- **Guest Networks:** Set up separate Wi-Fi networks for guests and employees. This prevents visitors from accessing internal systems while still providing internet access.

### 3.3 Secure Remote Access with Multi-Factor Authentication (MFA)

For remote access to network resources, always implement **Multi-Factor Authentication (MFA)** to add an extra layer of security.

- **MFA for VPN Access:** Require employees to use MFA when connecting to the corporate network via VPN. This helps ensure that only authorized users can access critical systems.
- **MFA for Cloud Services:** For cloud-based systems, enable MFA to secure access to corporate data and applications, especially when employees access them from remote locations.

---

## 4.

Building a secure network is a fundamental part of an organization's cybersecurity strategy. By implementing key strategies like defense in depth, network redundancy, strong access controls, and segmentation, organizations can greatly reduce the risk of cyberattacks, data breaches, and operational disruptions. Securing communication channels through encryption and remote access with MFA further strengthens network security. Following these best practices ensures that an organization's network is resilient, well-protected, and capable of supporting secure operations in today's digital landscape.

# Chapter 13: Wi-Fi Security

## *Overview*

Wi-Fi networks are essential for modern communication, offering convenient internet access for both personal and professional use. However, they can also be a significant vulnerability if not properly secured. Unsecured Wi-Fi networks, whether at home or in public places, can expose sensitive data to cybercriminals, who may intercept traffic, gain unauthorized access to devices, or launch attacks. This chapter discusses the risks of unsecured Wi-Fi networks and provides essential steps to secure your Wi-Fi both at home and in public places.

---

## 1. Risks of Unsecured Wi-Fi Networks

Unsecured or poorly secured Wi-Fi networks are highly vulnerable to various types of cyberattacks. Below are some of the most common risks associated with unsecured Wi-Fi networks:

### *1.1 Data Interception (Eavesdropping)*

When connected to an unsecured Wi-Fi network, your data can be intercepted by anyone within range of the network. This is particularly dangerous when transmitting sensitive information, such as login credentials, personal messages, or financial data.

- **Example:** A hacker in a coffee shop may set up a rogue Wi-Fi hotspot with a name similar to the legitimate one, hoping unsuspecting users will connect. Once connected, the attacker can intercept the data flowing between the device and the network.

## 1.2 Man-in-the-Middle (MITM) Attacks

In a MITM attack, an attacker secretly intercepts and alters communication between two parties without their knowledge. On an unsecured Wi-Fi network, attackers can alter the data being transmitted between users and websites, potentially injecting malicious content, stealing passwords, or redirecting users to phishing websites.

- **Example:** While using public Wi-Fi in an airport, an attacker intercepts your login credentials as you sign into your online banking account. The attacker can now access your account, posing a serious security risk.

## 1.3 Unauthorized Network Access

If your Wi-Fi network is unsecured or improperly configured, unauthorized users can gain access to your network. This opens the door for cybercriminals to monitor your online activities, access shared files, or exploit your internet connection for illegal activities.

- **Example:** If a neighbor or nearby individual gains access to your Wi-Fi network without permission, they could monitor your online activities or use your internet connection to download illegal content, making you liable.

### *1.4 Exploiting Devices on Your Network*

Once an attacker gains access to your Wi-Fi network, they can scan for vulnerable devices, such as printers, cameras, or smart home systems. Exploiting unsecured devices can lead to data theft, identity theft, or unauthorized control over your devices.

- **Example:** An attacker could exploit a weakly secured smart home system to unlock doors, control surveillance cameras, or hijack a voice-controlled assistant to listen in on private conversations.

## 2. Steps to Secure Your Wi-Fi at Home

### *2.1 Use Strong Wi-Fi Encryption*

Ensure your Wi-Fi network is encrypted using WPA3 (Wi-Fi Protected Access 3) or at least WPA2. These encryption protocols secure data transmitted over your network by converting it into unreadable code, preventing unauthorized users from accessing or intercepting your traffic.

- **How to Enable WPA2/WPA3 Encryption:**

o  Log in to your router's admin page (usually accessible by typing the router's IP address into a web browser).
o  Locate the wireless security settings section.
o  Choose WPA3 (if available) or WPA2 as the encryption method.
o  Set a strong password for your Wi-Fi network.

## 2.2 Set a Strong Wi-Fi Password

Your Wi-Fi password should be long, unique, and complex. Avoid using common phrases, personal information (e.g., your name, birthdate), or easily guessable words. A strong password should contain a combination of uppercase and lowercase letters, numbers, and special characters.

- **Example:** A strong password could be T7g$k2Jz@l9V!qD7— a mix of letters, numbers, and symbols that would be extremely difficult for an attacker to guess.

## 2.3 Disable WPS (Wi-Fi Protected Setup)

Wi-Fi Protected Setup (WPS) is a feature that allows users to easily connect devices to a Wi-Fi network by pressing a button on the router or entering a PIN. While convenient, WPS has known vulnerabilities that hackers can exploit to gain access to your network.

- **How to Disable WPS:**

- o Access your router's admin interface.
- o Navigate to the WPS settings section and disable it.

## *2.4 Change Default Router Credentials*

Many routers come with default admin usernames and passwords that are widely known or easily guessable. Change the default login credentials for your router to something unique and secure to prevent unauthorized access to your router's settings.

- **How to Change Default Router Credentials:**
  - o Log in to your router's admin page.
  - o Locate the settings for the admin username and password.
  - o Set a strong, unique password that's different from the default.

## *2.5 Enable a Guest Network*

If you frequently have visitors or guests who need to access your Wi-Fi, set up a **guest network**. This network should be isolated from your main network, preventing guests from accessing your personal devices or data.

- **How to Set Up a Guest Network:**
  - o Access your router's admin page.
  - o Navigate to the Wi-Fi settings section.
  - o Enable the guest network option and configure a separate password for guests.

    o   Ensure that the guest network has no access to the main network.

### 2.6 Regularly Update Router Firmware

Router manufacturers frequently release firmware updates to fix security vulnerabilities, improve performance, and enhance features. Regularly updating your router's firmware ensures that you're protected against known vulnerabilities.

- **How to Update Router Firmware:**
    - Log in to your router's admin page.
    - Check for available firmware updates in the router's settings section.
    - Follow the on-screen instructions to update your router firmware.

---

## 3. Steps to Secure Wi-Fi in Public Places

Public Wi-Fi networks, such as those in coffee shops, airports, and hotels, present unique security risks. Because these networks are typically unsecured and open to anyone, they are prime targets for cybercriminals.

### 3.1 Use a VPN (Virtual Private Network)

When using public Wi-Fi, a **VPN** encrypts your internet traffic, making it unreadable to anyone attempting to intercept it. This is one of the most effective ways to protect your privacy and data on public networks.

- **How to Use a VPN:**
  - Choose a reputable VPN provider (e.g., NordVPN, ExpressVPN, or CyberGhost).
  - Install the VPN software on your device and connect to a secure VPN server before using public Wi-Fi.
  - The VPN will encrypt all data sent over the Wi-Fi network, providing secure access to websites, email, and other online services.

### 3.2 Avoid Accessing Sensitive Information

When connected to public Wi-Fi, avoid accessing sensitive accounts, such as online banking, entering passwords, or making purchases. Public networks are more likely to be targeted by hackers using man-in-the-middle attacks to capture login credentials or financial information.

- **Example:** Avoid logging into your bank account or entering your credit card details when connected to a public Wi-Fi network.

### 3.3 Turn Off Sharing Features

Most devices come with file sharing and network discovery features that allow other users on the same network to access files or printers. When using public Wi-Fi, turn off these features to reduce the risk of unauthorized access.

- **How to Turn Off File Sharing:**
  - On Windows: Go to **Control Panel → Network and Sharing Center → Change advanced sharing settings** and turn off file and printer sharing.
  - On macOS: Go to **System Preferences → Sharing** and disable file sharing and other unnecessary services.

## 3.4 Use HTTPS and Secure Websites

Always ensure that the websites you visit use **HTTPS** (Hypertext Transfer Protocol Secure), which encrypts the data exchanged between your device and the website. This adds an extra layer of security, making it harder for attackers to intercept sensitive information.

- **How to Check for HTTPS:**
  - Look for a padlock icon in the browser's address bar, indicating that the website uses SSL/TLS encryption.

## 3.5 Forget the Network After Use

After using public Wi-Fi, ensure that your device **forgets** the network. This prevents it from automatically connecting to the same network in the future without your knowledge.

- **How to Forget a Network:**
  - On Windows: Go to **Settings** → **Network & Internet** → **Wi-Fi** → **Manage known networks** and remove the public network.
  - On macOS: Go to **System Preferences** → **Network** → **Wi-Fi** → **Advanced** and remove the public network from the list.

## 4.

Securing your Wi-Fi network is a critical part of protecting your digital privacy and ensuring that your personal and organizational data remains safe. Whether you're securing Wi-Fi at home or using public networks, implementing basic security measures—such as enabling encryption, setting strong passwords, and using VPNs—can significantly reduce the risk of cyberattacks and unauthorized access. By following the best practices outlined in this chapter, you can create a safer online environment for yourself and your organization, even when connected to unsecured networks.

# Chapter 14: Data Encryption: Protecting Data in Transit and at Rest

*Overview*

Data encryption is a cornerstone of modern cybersecurity practices, providing robust protection for sensitive information both in transit (while being transferred across networks) and at rest (when stored on servers, databases, or devices). By converting data into an unreadable format, encryption ensures that only authorized parties with the correct decryption key can access the data. This chapter delves into how encryption works, its role in data protection, and how to implement encryption tools to secure data effectively.

---

## 1. How Encryption Works and Its Role in Data Protection

Encryption is the process of converting readable data into an unreadable format using a mathematical algorithm and a key. The primary goal of encryption is to protect data from unauthorized access, ensuring confidentiality, integrity, and security. Encrypted data can only be decrypted and converted back into its original form by someone possessing the appropriate decryption key.

*1.1 The Basics of Encryption*

- **Plaintext:** This is the original, readable data that is inputted into an encryption algorithm.
- **Ciphertext:** The encrypted version of the data, which is unreadable without decryption.
- **Encryption Algorithm:** A mathematical function used to transform plaintext into ciphertext. Popular encryption algorithms include AES (Advanced Encryption Standard), RSA (Rivest-Shamir-Adleman), and Triple DES.
- **Encryption Key:** A string of characters used by the algorithm to transform plaintext into ciphertext. The key must be kept secure, as possession of the key allows decryption.

## 1.2 Types of Encryption

There are two main types of encryption: **symmetric encryption** and **asymmetric encryption**.

- **Symmetric Encryption:** In symmetric encryption, the same key is used for both encryption and decryption. The key must be shared securely between the sender and recipient.
  - o **Example: AES (Advanced Encryption Standard)** is one of the most commonly used symmetric encryption algorithms, providing a high level of security for both data in transit and at rest.
- **Asymmetric Encryption:** Asymmetric encryption uses two different keys—one for encryption (public key) and another

for decryption (private key). The public key can be shared openly, while the private key is kept secret.

- ○ **Example: RSA** is a widely used asymmetric encryption algorithm, where a public key is used to encrypt data, and only the private key can decrypt it. This is commonly used in secure communication channels like email and websites.

## *1.3 Role of Encryption in Data Protection*

- **Confidentiality:** Encryption ensures that only authorized users can access sensitive data, protecting it from unauthorized access by hackers or malicious actors.
- **Integrity:** Encryption helps ensure that the data remains unaltered during transmission. If data is tampered with, it cannot be decrypted properly, alerting the recipient to potential breaches.
- **Authentication:** Encryption provides a mechanism for verifying the identity of parties involved in communication. With asymmetric encryption, the sender's identity can be confirmed by decrypting data with a public key, ensuring that the message truly comes from the claimed source.
- **Non-repudiation:** In many cases, encryption ensures that the sender cannot deny having sent the data, as the encrypted message can only come from the sender with access to the private key.

## 2. Implementing Encryption Tools for Data Security

### 2.1 Encrypting Data in Transit

Data in transit is data actively being transferred across a network, such as data being sent over the internet, email, or within a corporate network. Encrypting data in transit protects it from being intercepted, read, or altered during transmission.

**Common Tools and Methods for Encrypting Data in Transit:**

1. **Transport Layer Security (TLS):**
   - **How it Works:** TLS is a protocol used to encrypt data transmitted over networks. It ensures that data sent over the internet (e.g., from a browser to a web server) is securely encrypted and cannot be intercepted by attackers.
   - **Use Cases:** TLS is widely used in HTTPS websites (secure websites) to encrypt communications between the user's browser and the website, ensuring that sensitive information like passwords and payment details remain private.
   - **Example:** When you access an online banking site, TLS encrypts the data between your browser and the bank's server, ensuring that your account information cannot be intercepted.

2. **Virtual Private Network (VPN):**

   o **How it Works:** A VPN creates a secure, encrypted tunnel between a device and a remote server, protecting all data transmitted over the connection from eavesdropping or interception.

   o **Use Cases:** VPNs are commonly used for secure remote access to corporate networks, as well as for maintaining privacy when browsing on public Wi-Fi.

   o **Example:** When employees access the corporate network from home, a VPN encrypts their internet traffic, protecting company data and communications from hackers.

3. **Secure File Transfer Protocols (SFTP/FTPS):**

   o **How it Works:** These protocols encrypt data during file transfers, ensuring that files are securely sent over the internet.

   o **Use Cases:** SFTP (Secure File Transfer Protocol) and FTPS (FTP Secure) are commonly used for transferring files containing sensitive information.

   o **Example:** A law firm might use SFTP to securely send confidential client documents to another office or external partners.

*2.2 Encrypting Data at Rest*

Data at rest refers to data stored on devices or storage systems, such as hard drives, servers, cloud storage, or databases. Encrypting data at rest ensures that even if the physical device is stolen or compromised, the data remains inaccessible without the encryption key.

**Common Tools and Methods for Encrypting Data at Rest:**

1. **Full Disk Encryption (FDE):**
   o **How it Works:** FDE encrypts the entire disk or hard drive, including the operating system, files, and applications. It ensures that all data stored on the device is encrypted automatically.
   o **Use Cases:** FDE is commonly used on laptops, desktops, and mobile devices to protect data in case the device is lost or stolen.
   o **Example: BitLocker** (Windows) and **FileVault** (macOS) are examples of full disk encryption tools that protect data on a laptop or desktop. These tools encrypt the entire disk, requiring a passcode or PIN to access the data.

2. **Database Encryption:**
   o **How it Works:** Database encryption involves encrypting the data stored in databases to protect it from unauthorized access. Only authorized users with the correct decryption key can access sensitive records.

- o **Use Cases:** Database encryption is commonly used to protect sensitive customer data, such as credit card numbers, personally identifiable information (PII), and financial records.

- o **Example: Transparent Data Encryption (TDE)** in SQL Server or **Oracle Advanced Security** is used to encrypt the data stored in databases automatically, protecting it from unauthorized access.

3. **File-Level Encryption:**

   - o **How it Works:** This method encrypts individual files or directories rather than the entire system or database, allowing organizations to encrypt only the most sensitive files.

   - o **Use Cases:** File-level encryption is useful when only certain files need protection, such as financial documents or confidential contracts.

   - o **Example: VeraCrypt** and **AxCrypt** are tools that allow users to encrypt specific files or folders. These tools can be used to protect sensitive documents before sharing or storing them.

# 3. Best Practices for Implementing Encryption

1. **Use Strong Encryption Algorithms:**

- o Always opt for well-established, strong encryption algorithms like **AES-256** (Advanced Encryption Standard with a 256-bit key) for both data at rest and in transit. Avoid outdated algorithms like **DES** (Data Encryption Standard) or **RC4**, which are no longer considered secure.

2. **Key Management:**
   - o Secure encryption keys are the backbone of the encryption process. Implement a robust **key management** system to store and protect encryption keys. Consider using **Hardware Security Modules (HSMs)** or **cloud-based key management services** (e.g., AWS KMS, Azure Key Vault) for secure key storage and rotation.
   - o **Best Practice:** Avoid storing encryption keys with encrypted data. Store keys in a separate, highly secure location to reduce the risk of both being compromised together.

3. **Regularly Update Encryption Protocols:**
   - o Encryption protocols evolve to address new vulnerabilities and threats. Regularly update your encryption tools and methods to ensure they remain secure. For example, transition from **SSL** to **TLS** for web encryption, and ensure that your systems are configured to support the latest security standards.

4. **Encrypt Backups:**
   - Encrypting backup copies of data is essential. Backups are often a target for attackers looking to steal or manipulate data, and encrypting them ensures that they are protected from unauthorized access.

5. **Monitor Encryption Effectiveness:**
   - Continuously monitor the effectiveness of encryption policies. Ensure that encryption is being applied uniformly across all devices and systems, and test encryption regularly to verify that there are no weaknesses or vulnerabilities in the implementation.

# 4.

Data encryption is a fundamental aspect of data security, ensuring that sensitive information remains protected both during transmission and while stored on devices or servers. Whether it's securing communications over the internet with TLS, encrypting files on a laptop with full disk encryption, or protecting data in the cloud with database encryption, encryption is essential for maintaining confidentiality, integrity, and compliance. By implementing strong encryption methods, utilizing robust key management practices, and following encryption best practices, organizations can safeguard their critical data from theft, breaches, and cyberattacks.

# Chapter 15: Backup and Recovery

*Overview*

Data is one of an organization's most valuable assets, and losing it—whether due to human error, hardware failure, cyberattacks, or natural disasters—can have catastrophic consequences. Regular data backups and a solid recovery plan are essential to mitigate the risks associated with data loss and ensure business continuity. This chapter explores the importance of regular data backups and provides best practices for backing up data and creating an effective disaster recovery plan.

---

## 1. The Importance of Regular Data Backups

### *1.1 Protecting Against Data Loss*

Data loss can occur for a variety of reasons, and the impact on organizations can be severe, ranging from operational disruption to reputational damage. Common causes of data loss include:

- **Hardware Failure:** Hard drives, servers, and storage devices can fail unexpectedly, leading to data loss.
- **Cyberattacks and Ransomware:** Attackers can corrupt, steal, or hold data hostage by encrypting it and demanding payment.

- **Human Error:** Accidental deletion or misplacement of data is a common cause of data loss.
- **Natural Disasters:** Floods, fires, earthquakes, and other disasters can physically damage servers or storage devices.

Without regular backups, organizations are vulnerable to significant data loss, making it difficult to recover critical information or resume operations.

### *1.2 Business Continuity and Downtime Prevention*

In addition to safeguarding data, regular backups are essential for maintaining **business continuity**. Downtime—whether caused by a cyberattack, natural disaster, or hardware failure—can result in lost revenue, missed deadlines, and a damaged reputation. A reliable backup system ensures that data can be quickly restored, minimizing downtime and enabling the organization to continue functioning even after an incident.

- **Example:** If a company's main database is corrupted by ransomware, having an up-to-date backup allows the company to restore the database to its previous state without paying the ransom.

### *1.3 Compliance and Legal Requirements*

Many industries are governed by strict data protection regulations (e.g., **GDPR**, **HIPAA**) that require organizations to implement certain data protection measures, including regular backups. Failing to meet these requirements can lead to legal penalties and loss of customer trust.

- **Example:** A healthcare provider must regularly back up patient records to comply with HIPAA regulations, ensuring that patient information remains secure and accessible even after a data breach or system failure.

---

## 2. Best Practices for Backing Up Data

### 2.1 Follow the 3-2-1 Backup Rule

The **3-2-1 backup rule** is a widely recommended best practice for ensuring data redundancy and availability:

1. **Three Copies of Data:** Keep three copies of your data—the original data and two backups.
2. **Two Different Media:** Store backups on two different types of media (e.g., external hard drives, cloud storage, or network-attached storage).
3. **One Offsite Copy:** Keep one backup copy offsite (e.g., in a cloud service or external location) to protect against local disasters (e.g., fire, theft, or flooding).

By adhering to the 3-2-1 rule, organizations can significantly reduce the risk of losing data due to hardware failure, natural disasters, or cyberattacks.

## 2.2 Automate Backups

Manual backups can be error-prone and easily forgotten, leading to gaps in your backup strategy. Automating backups ensures that they occur regularly and without human intervention.

- **How to Automate Backups:**
    - **Cloud Backups:** Many cloud services, such as **Google Drive**, **Dropbox**, or **OneDrive**, offer automatic syncing and backup features. For businesses, cloud providers like **AWS**, **Azure**, and **Google Cloud** offer enterprise-grade backup solutions.
    - **Backup Software:** Tools like **Acronis**, **Veeam**, and **Backblaze** allow you to schedule automatic backups of files, databases, and even entire systems.

Automating backups reduces the risk of forgetting to perform them, ensuring that your data is consistently backed up and up-to-date.

## 2.3 Perform Regular Backup Testing

A backup is only useful if it can be successfully restored when needed. Regular testing of backups ensures that the data is intact, accessible, and free from corruption.

- **How to Test Backups:**
  - ○ Periodically perform **test restores** of your backup data to verify that the process works smoothly and that the data can be accessed or restored to a working state.
  - ○ Test both **full-system backups** and **file-level backups** to ensure that both types of backup can be successfully restored in the event of a disaster.

## *2.4 Use Encryption for Backup Files*

Data backups can become a target for hackers. Encrypting backup files ensures that even if they are stolen or accessed by unauthorized individuals, they cannot be read without the decryption key.

- **How to Encrypt Backup Files:**
  - ○ Use **encryption tools** built into backup software (e.g., **Veeam, Acronis, Windows Backup**) or third-party encryption tools (e.g., **VeraCrypt, BitLocker**) to encrypt backup files.
  - ○ Ensure that encryption keys are securely stored and not left with the backup data itself to prevent unauthorized decryption.

## *2.5 Back Up Critical Data Frequently*

The frequency of backups should be determined by the value and importance of the data. Critical data (e.g., financial records, customer data, and intellectual property) should be backed up more frequently than less important files (e.g., archived documents).

- **How to Schedule Backups:**
  - **Critical Data:** Perform backups on a **daily** or even **hourly** basis to ensure the most up-to-date copy of important data.
  - **Less Critical Data:** Schedule backups for non-essential files on a **weekly** or **monthly** basis.

## 3. Creating a Disaster Recovery Plan

A **disaster recovery plan (DRP)** outlines the steps an organization will take to recover from a disaster, such as data loss, hardware failure, or cyberattack. The goal of a DRP is to minimize downtime and ensure the organization can quickly restore critical services and systems.

### 3.1 Identify Critical Systems and Data

To create an effective DRP, identify which systems, applications, and data are most critical to the operation of your business. These are the systems that require the highest priority during recovery.

- **Critical Data:** Customer information, financial records, intellectual property, and any other data vital to the organization's operations.
- **Critical Systems:** Databases, email servers, file servers, and any other infrastructure that is crucial for business continuity.

## *3.2 Define Recovery Objectives*

Two key metrics help determine the scope and timeline for recovery:

1. **Recovery Time Objective (RTO):** The maximum acceptable time it takes to restore a system or data after a disaster. For example, a company may aim for an RTO of four hours for their email server.

2. **Recovery Point Objective (RPO):** The maximum acceptable amount of data loss, measured in time. For example, a company may aim for an RPO of one hour, meaning it can tolerate losing up to one hour's worth of data.

## *3.3 Document Recovery Procedures*

Your DRP should include detailed procedures for recovering data and systems in the event of a disaster. These procedures should be specific to the types of disasters your organization might face (e.g., hardware failure, ransomware attack, natural disaster).

- **Steps in the Recovery Process:**
    1. **Identify the cause of the disruption** (e.g., hardware failure, cyberattack).

2. **Activate the disaster recovery team** and notify stakeholders.

3. **Restore from backups** according to the priority list of systems and data.

4. **Test the restored systems** to ensure they are functioning properly before bringing them back online.

### *3.4 Regularly Review and Update the Disaster Recovery Plan*

The DRP should be reviewed and updated regularly to account for changes in business operations, technology, or potential threats. Additionally, as new data, systems, and applications are added, the recovery plan should be adjusted accordingly.

- **Review and Testing:** Regularly test the disaster recovery plan by simulating different disaster scenarios (e.g., ransomware attack, server crash) to ensure that recovery procedures are effective and that recovery times meet business objectives.

---

## 4.

Regular data backups and a well-structured disaster recovery plan are essential for ensuring business continuity in the face of unexpected disruptions. By following best practices for backup, such as using the 3-2-1 rule, automating backups, and testing backup integrity, organizations can minimize the impact of data loss and quickly restore operations. Furthermore, an up-to-date disaster recovery plan helps ensure that critical systems and data are restored in a timely manner, reducing downtime and protecting the organization's reputation. Ultimately, investing in effective backup and recovery strategies strengthens the organization's resilience against data loss and cyber threats.

# Chapter 16: Securing Cloud Storage

## *Overview*

Cloud storage has become an essential part of modern business and personal data management, offering scalability, flexibility, and convenience. However, as more organizations and individuals rely on cloud services to store sensitive data, it's critical to understand the risks associated with these services and how to secure cloud storage to prevent unauthorized access and data breaches. This chapter explores the risks of cloud storage and cloud services, and provides guidance on how to secure cloud storage with encryption and access controls.

---

## 1. Risks Associated with Cloud Storage and Cloud Services

While cloud storage offers numerous benefits, it also introduces unique security risks that must be addressed to ensure that data remains protected.

### *1.1 Data Breaches*

Cloud storage is a prime target for cybercriminals due to the valuable data it holds. A data breach can expose sensitive personal, financial, and corporate data, leading to identity theft, financial loss, and reputational damage.

- **Example:** Hackers gain access to an organization's cloud storage due to weak passwords or poor security configurations, stealing sensitive customer data such as credit card numbers or personal identification details.

## *1.2 Data Loss*

Cloud storage providers offer high levels of redundancy, but there's always the risk of data loss due to service outages, human error, or malicious attacks. If a cloud service provider experiences technical failures or is targeted by a cyberattack, it could lead to the permanent loss of stored data.

- **Example:** A cloud provider accidentally deletes or corrupts client data, and the client's backup strategy is inadequate, leading to the loss of critical business files.

## *1.3 Inadequate Access Controls*

Cloud storage services often provide easy access to data from any device with an internet connection, but without strong access controls, unauthorized users or malicious insiders could gain access to sensitive data.

- **Example:** A company's cloud storage is configured with broad access permissions, allowing employees and external contractors to access sensitive information, leading to potential data leaks or misuse.

### 1.4 Insider Threats

Insider threats—whether intentional or accidental—pose a significant risk in cloud environments. Employees, contractors, or service providers with legitimate access to cloud storage can abuse their privileges to steal or leak sensitive data.

- **Example:** A disgruntled employee with access to company cloud storage deliberately downloads or shares confidential business data with competitors or the public.

### 1.5 Shared Responsibility Model

In the cloud, security is often a shared responsibility between the cloud provider and the customer. While the cloud provider is responsible for securing the physical infrastructure, the customer is responsible for securing data, access, and configuration.

- **Example:** A cloud provider may secure the data center, but it's up to the organization to ensure that their data in the cloud is encrypted, access is controlled, and permissions are set correctly.

### 1.6 Lack of Compliance

Organizations that use cloud services to store sensitive data, such as healthcare or financial information, may face compliance challenges. Depending on the industry, regulations like **GDPR**, **HIPAA**, and **PCI-DSS** require organizations to implement specific controls to protect data.

- **Example:** A company stores customer health records in the cloud without ensuring that the cloud provider complies with **HIPAA** regulations, potentially leading to non-compliance penalties.

---

# 2. How to Secure Cloud Storage with Encryption and Access Controls

Securing data stored in the cloud requires a combination of encryption, access controls, and other best practices to protect against unauthorized access and mitigate the risks mentioned above.

## 2.1 Using Encryption to Protect Data

Encryption is one of the most effective ways to protect data in cloud storage. It ensures that even if attackers gain access to stored data, they will not be able to read it without the decryption key.

**Types of Encryption for Cloud Storage:**

1. **Data at Rest Encryption:**
   - Data at rest refers to data stored on physical media, such as databases or cloud storage. Encrypting data at rest ensures that data is unreadable while it is stored in the cloud, preventing unauthorized access.

- o **How to Implement:** Enable encryption through the cloud provider's settings or use third-party encryption tools. Many cloud providers, such as **Amazon Web Services (AWS)** and **Google Cloud**, offer built-in encryption options for data stored on their servers.

2. **Data in Transit Encryption:**
   - o Data in transit refers to data being transmitted over networks (e.g., uploading or downloading files from the cloud). Encrypting data in transit ensures that data is protected as it moves between devices and cloud servers.
   - o **How to Implement:** Ensure that all data transferred between your devices and cloud storage is encrypted using **SSL/TLS** (Secure Sockets Layer/Transport Layer Security). Most reputable cloud storage providers use SSL/TLS encryption by default.

3. **Client-Side Encryption:**
   - o In client-side encryption, data is encrypted on the user's device before it is uploaded to the cloud, and only the user holds the decryption key. This approach ensures that the cloud provider cannot access the data.
   - o **How to Implement:** Use third-party tools like **Cryptomator** or **Boxcryptor** to encrypt files on your device before uploading them to the cloud.

4. **End-to-End Encryption:**

   o End-to-end encryption ensures that data is encrypted on the sender's side and only decrypted on the recipient's side, meaning no one else— including the cloud service provider—can read the data while it is being stored or transmitted.

   o **How to Implement:** Choose cloud services that offer end-to-end encryption, or use third-party tools that enable this feature, such as **Tresorit** or **Sync.com**.

## 2.2 Implementing Access Controls

Effective access control mechanisms ensure that only authorized users can access cloud data and resources. Implementing strong access controls minimizes the risk of unauthorized access or misuse of data.

1. **Use Strong Authentication Methods:**

   o **Multi-Factor Authentication (MFA):** MFA is one of the most effective ways to secure cloud accounts. With MFA, users must provide two or more forms of authentication (e.g., password and a one-time code sent to their phone) before they can access data.

   ▪ **How to Implement:** Enable MFA for all users who access cloud storage. Most cloud providers offer built-in MFA options, including SMS-based authentication or authentication apps like **Google Authenticator** or **Authy**.

2. **Role-Based Access Control (RBAC):**

   o RBAC assigns permissions based on a user's role within the organization, ensuring that employees only have access to the data necessary for their job functions. By limiting access to sensitive data, organizations can reduce the risk of unauthorized access.

     ▪ **How to Implement:** Set up roles (e.g., Admin, User, Manager) within the cloud platform, and assign data access permissions based on these roles. For example, a marketing employee may only have access to marketing materials, not financial records.

3. **Least Privilege Principle:**

   o The principle of least privilege states that users and applications should be granted the minimum level of access necessary to perform their tasks. Limiting access to sensitive data helps mitigate the impact of insider threats and data breaches.

     ▪ **How to Implement:** Regularly audit user access levels and remove any unnecessary permissions. Restrict the ability to download, modify, or share data based on user roles.

4. **Use of Identity and Access Management (IAM) Systems:**
   o IAM systems help manage user identities and their access to cloud resources. These systems allow administrators to define access policies, authenticate users, and enforce security controls across multiple cloud services.
      - **How to Implement:** Use cloud providers' built-in IAM solutions, such as **AWS IAM**, **Azure Active Directory**, or **Google Cloud IAM**, to manage and enforce user access policies.

5. **Audit Logs and Monitoring:**
   o Regular monitoring and logging of user activity are critical for detecting unauthorized access or suspicious behavior within the cloud environment. Maintaining detailed logs can help with compliance, troubleshooting, and incident response.
      - **How to Implement:** Enable logging and continuous monitoring for cloud accounts and set up alerts for unusual access patterns (e.g., multiple failed login attempts or access to sensitive files).

## *2.3 Backup and Disaster Recovery*

Data stored in the cloud can be lost or corrupted due to cyberattacks, accidental deletion, or natural disasters. Implementing strong backup and recovery mechanisms ensures that data can be restored in the event of an incident.

- **Backup Best Practices:** Ensure that your cloud data is regularly backed up to an offsite or secondary location. Cloud providers often offer backup solutions, but consider using a third-party tool to automate and secure your backup process.
- **Disaster Recovery:** Implement a disaster recovery plan that defines how to restore cloud data and systems in the event of an outage or data breach. This plan should include specific recovery points, testing procedures, and roles and responsibilities.

---

## 3.

Securing cloud storage is essential to safeguarding sensitive data and ensuring business continuity in the face of cyber threats, data breaches, and accidental loss. By leveraging encryption, access controls, and effective backup and recovery strategies, organizations can significantly enhance the security of their cloud environments. Regularly reviewing security policies, implementing the principle of least privilege, and using strong authentication methods like multi-factor authentication (MFA) are crucial for maintaining robust protection against unauthorized access. By following these best practices, organizations can confidently use cloud storage while mitigating risks associated with data security.

# Chapter 17: Understanding Identity and Access Management (IAM)

*Overview*

Identity and Access Management (IAM) is a critical framework used to ensure that the right individuals have the appropriate access to resources within an organization. IAM solutions help manage user identities, enforce policies, and control access permissions to ensure that sensitive data and systems are protected. As businesses increasingly adopt cloud services, remote work, and more complex IT infrastructures, IAM becomes essential for safeguarding digital environments. This chapter explores how IAM helps manage users, identities, and permissions, and discusses common tools and strategies used in IAM.

---

## 1. How IAM Helps Manage Users, Identities, and Permissions

### 1.1 What is Identity and Access Management (IAM)?

**Identity and Access Management (IAM)** refers to a set of policies, technologies, and processes that ensure that only authorized individuals can access specific resources, applications, and data within an organization. IAM enables administrators to define user roles, enforce access policies, and track user activity to minimize the risk of unauthorized access or misuse of critical systems.

Key components of IAM include:

- **User Identity:** The unique identification of each user within an organization, typically tied to their login credentials (username, password, etc.).
- **Authentication:** The process of verifying that a user is who they claim to be, usually by requiring a password, biometric scan, or multi-factor authentication (MFA).
- **Authorization:** The process of granting or denying access to specific resources based on the user's identity, role, or permissions.
- **Access Control Policies:** Rules that dictate which users can access which resources, and under what conditions.

### 1.2 Managing User Identities

IAM systems maintain a central repository of user identities and associated attributes (e.g., name, email, role, department). This centralized management simplifies the process of onboarding, offboarding, and managing user access across multiple systems and applications.

- **User Creation and Modification:** When a new employee joins, their identity is created in the IAM system. When an employee changes roles or leaves, their access is updated or revoked accordingly.

- **Identity Federation:** IAM solutions can link identities across multiple organizations or platforms. This is particularly useful for organizations that collaborate with external partners or use multiple cloud services.

### *1.3 Authentication and Single Sign-On (SSO)*

Authentication is a key component of IAM, ensuring that users are verified before accessing resources. A common IAM practice is **Single Sign-On (SSO)**, which allows users to authenticate once and access multiple applications or systems without needing to log in again for each service.

- **Example:** A user logs in to their corporate network using their credentials and can then access their email, CRM system, and cloud storage without having to log in separately to each service.

### *1.4 Authorization and Role-Based Access Control (RBAC)*

Once a user is authenticated, IAM determines what actions they can perform through **authorization** mechanisms. The most common model used for controlling access is **Role-Based Access Control (RBAC)**, where users are assigned roles (e.g., admin, manager, employee) and granted access based on their roles.

- **Example:** An employee in the finance department may have access to financial records, while an employee in the marketing department would only have access to marketing-related data.

## *1.5 Privilege Management*

Managing user privileges ensures that users have the minimum level of access necessary to perform their tasks. This is referred to as the **principle of least privilege** (PoLP), which reduces the risk of unauthorized access and limits the impact of potential security breaches.

- **Example:** A support staff member may need access to basic user data to troubleshoot issues but should not have access to financial data or other sensitive information.

---

# 2. Common Tools and Strategies Used in IAM

To implement IAM effectively, organizations rely on various tools and strategies that help automate user management, improve security, and ensure compliance with regulations.

## *2.1 IAM Solutions and Platforms*

1. **Cloud-Based IAM Solutions:** Cloud-based IAM solutions enable organizations to manage user identities and access for

cloud-based services and applications, often with a central platform that integrates with other cloud services. These tools are particularly valuable for businesses adopting hybrid or multi-cloud environments.

- o **Examples:**
  - **Okta:** A widely used IAM platform that offers SSO, MFA, and lifecycle management for both on-premises and cloud-based applications.
  - **Microsoft Azure Active Directory (Azure AD):** A cloud-based IAM service that provides identity management and access control for Microsoft services and third-party applications.

2. **On-Premises IAM Solutions:** On-premises IAM solutions are used by organizations that require more control over their IAM systems, often for compliance or privacy reasons. These solutions can be customized for specific use cases but often require more resources to maintain and scale.

- o **Examples:**
  - **Microsoft Active Directory (AD):** A traditional on-premises solution widely used for managing user accounts, groups, and security policies within a local network.

- **IBM Security Identity Governance and Administration:** Provides comprehensive IAM solutions for managing user identities, roles, and access permissions across on-premises systems.

3. **Identity as a Service (IDaaS):** IDaaS is a cloud-based IAM solution that delivers identity and access management functions as a service, allowing businesses to offload IAM management to a third-party provider.

   o **Examples:**

     - **OneLogin:** An IDaaS provider that offers SSO, MFA, and user provisioning for cloud applications and on-premises services.
     - **Ping Identity:** Provides secure identity solutions, including SSO, MFA, and identity federation, for organizations with complex IT infrastructures.

### 2.2 Multi-Factor Authentication (MFA)

**Multi-Factor Authentication (MFA)** enhances security by requiring multiple forms of authentication before granting access to a system. This typically involves something the user knows (e.g., a password), something the user has (e.g., a phone or hardware token), and/or something the user is (e.g., biometric data).

- **Example:** An employee must enter their password and then provide a code sent to their phone (SMS or app-based) before accessing the organization's sensitive data.

### 2.3 Single Sign-On (SSO)

Single Sign-On (SSO) allows users to authenticate once and gain access to multiple applications and services without needing to log in repeatedly. SSO enhances user convenience and reduces the likelihood of weak passwords or reused credentials.

- **Example:** An employee logs into their organization's HR system, which also automatically grants them access to other applications like email, file storage, and customer relationship management (CRM) systems.

### 2.4 Identity Federation

Identity federation enables organizations to extend their IAM policies across multiple systems, services, and organizations. This is especially useful for businesses that partner with other organizations or use multiple cloud providers.

- **Example:** An employee from Company A needs to access an application hosted by Company B. Through identity federation, Company A's IAM system can authenticate the user and grant access to the application without requiring a separate login.

## *2.5 Privileged Access Management (PAM)*

Privileged Access Management (PAM) involves the management of privileged accounts (e.g., system administrators, root accounts) that have elevated permissions. These accounts are often targeted by attackers, making it essential to monitor and control access to them closely.

- **How to Implement PAM:**
  - o Use **privileged session management tools** to monitor and log all actions taken by privileged users.
  - o Apply **just-in-time access** to ensure that elevated privileges are granted only when necessary and for the shortest time possible.
  - o Implement **least privilege** for privileged accounts, ensuring they only have access to the systems and data necessary for their role.

---

# 3. Strategies for Implementing IAM Effectively

## *3.1 Establish Clear Access Policies*

Create detailed **access policies** that define who has access to what resources, when, and under what conditions. These policies should align with the organization's business needs and security requirements. Regularly review and update access policies as the organization's needs evolve.

- **Example:** An access policy may restrict access to financial data only to employees in the finance department and only during business hours.

### 3.2 Conduct Regular Access Audits

Regularly auditing user access is essential for identifying over-privileged accounts, ensuring compliance, and mitigating risks. Automated tools can assist in auditing user activities and detecting any unusual access patterns.

- **Example:** An audit might reveal that an employee in marketing has access to the finance system, which should be restricted. The IAM system can generate alerts to flag such discrepancies.

### 3.3 Enforce Strong Password Policies

Implement a strong **password policy** that requires users to set complex, unique passwords for their accounts. Use tools to enforce password strength requirements and periodic password changes.

- **Example:** A password policy might require a combination of upper and lower case letters, numbers, special characters, and a minimum length of 12 characters.

### 3.4 Provide User Education and Training

Educate users about the importance of IAM practices, such as using strong passwords, recognizing phishing attempts, and enabling

MFA. Employee awareness and involvement are crucial for maintaining a secure IAM environment.

- **Example:** Train employees to recognize phishing emails attempting to steal login credentials and how to securely store their passwords using a password manager.

---

Identity and Access Management (IAM) is a critical component of an organization's cybersecurity strategy. By managing user identities, roles, and access permissions, IAM helps ensure that only authorized users can access sensitive data and systems, reducing the risk of unauthorized access, data breaches, and insider threats. The adoption of tools like **MFA**, **SSO**, and **PAM**, combined with effective access policies and regular audits, enables organizations to implement robust IAM practices. As businesses continue to expand their digital footprint, implementing an effective IAM strategy is essential for protecting both user data and organizational assets.

# Chapter 18: Multi-Factor Authentication (MFA)

*Overview*

As cyber threats continue to evolve, securing user accounts with only a password is no longer sufficient. **Multi-Factor Authentication (MFA)** is a critical security measure that significantly enhances the protection of online accounts by requiring multiple forms of verification before granting access. This chapter explains the role of MFA in strengthening security and provides guidance on how to implement MFA across various types of accounts and devices.

## 1. The Role of MFA in Strengthening Security

### 1.1 What is Multi-Factor Authentication (MFA)?

Multi-Factor Authentication (MFA) is a security protocol that requires users to provide two or more verification factors when accessing an account or system. Instead of relying solely on something you know (like a password), MFA combines multiple authentication methods to verify a user's identity. The goal of MFA is to enhance security by adding layers of defense, making it significantly more difficult for unauthorized users to gain access to sensitive data or systems.

## *1.2 Types of Authentication Factors*

MFA typically involves at least two of the following factors:

1. **Something You Know:**
   - This is typically a **password** or **PIN**. It is the most common form of authentication but can be vulnerable to attacks like brute-force or phishing.
   - **Example:** Your account password or passcode.

2. **Something You Have:**
   - This involves physical objects, such as a **smartphone**, **security token**, or **smartcard**, that can generate a unique code for verification.
   - **Example:** A smartphone app like **Google Authenticator** or **Authy** that generates a time-based one-time password (TOTP).

3. **Something You Are:**
   - This refers to biometric factors such as **fingerprints**, **face recognition**, or **iris scans**, which are used to verify the user's identity based on unique physical characteristics.
   - **Example:** Using **Face ID** or **Touch ID** on an iPhone or **Windows Hello** on a Windows device.

4. **Something You Do:**
   - This can involve behavior-based biometrics, such as **typing patterns** or **mouse movements**, that are used to verify a user based on their actions.

o **Example:** Analyzing a user's typing speed or unique patterns while interacting with a device.

### 1.3 Why MFA is Critical for Strengthening Security

Passwords are often compromised through common tactics such as phishing, brute-force attacks, or social engineering. Even strong, complex passwords can be vulnerable if they are reused across multiple sites or if an attacker gains access through other means. MFA adds an additional layer of security that mitigates the risk of password theft by requiring at least one other verification factor.

- **Example:** If an attacker steals your password, they still cannot access your account unless they also have access to the second factor, such as your phone or a biometric feature.

### 1.4 Benefits of MFA

1. **Enhanced Security:** By requiring multiple factors for authentication, MFA makes it much harder for attackers to gain access, even if they have compromised a password.
2. **Protection Against Common Attacks:** MFA helps protect against common threats such as phishing, credential stuffing, and keylogging.
3. **Compliance with Regulations:** Many industries, such as healthcare and finance, have specific regulations (e.g., **HIPAA, PCI-DSS**) that require the use of MFA to protect sensitive data.

4.  **User Confidence:** Users feel more secure knowing that their accounts are protected by more than just a password.

---

## 2. How to Implement MFA for Different Types of Accounts and Devices

Implementing MFA across various accounts and devices adds layers of protection to an organization's digital environment. Below are the steps and best practices for setting up MFA on different types of accounts and devices.

### 2.1 Implementing MFA for Online Accounts

Online accounts, especially those associated with sensitive data, should have MFA enabled to protect against unauthorized access.

1.  **Email Accounts (e.g., Gmail, Outlook)**
    - **Google Gmail:**
        - Go to **Google Account Settings → Security → 2-Step Verification**.
        - Follow the prompts to set up a secondary authentication method, such as Google Authenticator, SMS, or a security key.
    - **Microsoft Outlook:**
        - Visit the **Microsoft Security Settings** page.

- Enable **Two-Step Verification** and follow the prompts to link a phone number or set up an authenticator app (like **Microsoft Authenticator**).

**Best Practice:** Use an authenticator app for a more secure and efficient method than SMS-based MFA, as SMS can be vulnerable to SIM swapping attacks.

2. **Social Media Accounts (e.g., Facebook, Twitter)**
   o **Facebook:**
     - Navigate to **Settings → Security and Login → Two-Factor Authentication**.
     - Choose the authentication method (e.g., text message, authenticator app, or Facebook's own security key).
   o **Twitter:**
     - Go to **Settings and Privacy → Security and Account Access → Security → Two-Factor Authentication**.
     - Twitter offers authentication via SMS, an authenticator app, or a physical security key.

**Best Practice:** Opt for app-based authentication over SMS for enhanced security and faster access.

3. **Financial and Payment Accounts (e.g., PayPal, Bank Accounts)**

    o **PayPal:**

        ▪ Go to **Settings** → **Security** → **Two-Factor Authentication**.

        ▪ PayPal supports both text message and app-based MFA.

    o **Banking Websites:**

        ▪ Most banks provide MFA in the form of either a text message, phone call, or dedicated mobile banking app.

        ▪ **Best Practice:** Use app-based MFA or hardware security tokens to protect financial transactions.

---

## 2.2 Implementing MFA for Corporate Networks

For organizations, securing access to corporate networks, cloud applications, and internal systems is paramount. Implementing MFA in corporate environments helps protect sensitive data and systems.

1. **Cloud Services (e.g., AWS, Google Cloud, Microsoft Azure)**

    o **AWS:**

- Enable **MFA** through the **IAM Console** to require MFA for accessing the AWS Management Console and other services.
- AWS supports virtual MFA devices (e.g., Google Authenticator) and hardware MFA devices (e.g., YubiKey).

  o **Google Cloud:**
    - Google Cloud IAM allows the integration of MFA with Google Cloud accounts. Admins can enforce MFA using **Google Authenticator** or **Security Keys**.

  o **Microsoft Azure:**
    - Azure Active Directory provides MFA integration across Azure services. It supports multiple factors, including phone calls, text messages, or mobile app notifications.

**Best Practice:** Implement conditional access policies in these platforms to enforce MFA based on user behavior, location, or the type of device being used.

2. **Corporate VPNs and Remote Access**
    o Implement MFA for VPN access to ensure that only authorized employees can connect to the corporate network remotely.

o **Best Practice:** Use **certificate-based authentication** along with MFA for added security, as it prevents unauthorized access even if login credentials are compromised.

3. **Enterprise Applications (e.g., Salesforce, Slack, Office 365)**

   o Most enterprise applications support MFA through integrations with identity providers (e.g., Azure AD, Okta) and MFA solutions (e.g., Duo Security).

   o **Best Practice:** Enforce MFA for accessing cloud applications like Salesforce or Office 365 to prevent unauthorized access to sensitive business data.

---

*2.3 Implementing MFA on Devices*

1. **Mobile Devices (e.g., Smartphones and Tablets)**

   o **iOS Devices (Apple):**

      ▪ Enable **Face ID** or **Touch ID** for device authentication. Additionally, turn on **Two-Factor Authentication** for your Apple ID to secure iCloud, App Store, and other Apple services.

   o **Android Devices:**

- Use **Google's two-step verification** for securing Google accounts. Additionally, Android devices can implement biometric authentication (fingerprint or face recognition) for unlocking the device.

**Best Practice:** Combine biometric authentication with a PIN or password for an added layer of security.

2. **Laptops and Desktop Devices**
   o **Windows 10/11:**
     - **Windows Hello** provides biometric authentication options such as facial recognition or fingerprint scanning.
     - Alternatively, enable **MFA** via Microsoft accounts or third-party solutions like **Duo Security** to secure login access.
   o **Mac OS:**
     - Use **Touch ID** for device unlocking and enable **Apple's two-factor authentication** for iCloud and Apple ID.

# 3. Best Practices for MFA Implementation

1. **Use MFA for All Critical Accounts**

o Always enable MFA on high-risk and sensitive accounts, such as email, financial accounts, cloud services, and corporate networks. The more critical the account, the higher the risk associated with it being compromised.

2. **Educate Users on MFA**

   o Train employees and users on the importance of MFA and how to set it up properly. Awareness and adherence to MFA policies are crucial for reducing vulnerabilities in the system.

3. **Use App-Based Authentication Over SMS**

   o While SMS-based MFA is convenient, it is more susceptible to SIM-swapping attacks. Encourage users to use app-based authentication (e.g., **Google Authenticator, Authy**, or **Microsoft Authenticator**) or hardware security keys for better protection.

4. **Regularly Review and Update MFA Policies**

   o Periodically audit user accounts and ensure that MFA is still active for high-risk accounts. Implement periodic reviews and updates to MFA settings, ensuring users are adhering to the latest security guidelines.

Multi-Factor Authentication (MFA) is one of the most effective ways to strengthen security and protect against unauthorized access. By requiring multiple forms of verification—something you know, something you have, and something you are—MFA ensures that even if one factor is compromised, the account remains secure. Implementing MFA across different types of accounts and devices enhances overall security and reduces the risk of cyberattacks. As cyber threats continue to grow in sophistication, adopting MFA as a core component of your security strategy is critical for safeguarding sensitive data, ensuring privacy, and maintaining trust in digital systems.

# Chapter 19: Password Security

*Overview*

Passwords are the first line of defense in protecting sensitive information, making password security critical for both individuals and organizations. However, as cyberattacks evolve, relying on weak passwords or reusing passwords across multiple platforms increases the risk of unauthorized access. This chapter explores how to create strong passwords, the importance of password managers, and best practices for password hygiene. Additionally, we discuss the significance of having password policies in place for businesses to prevent security breaches.

---

# 1. Creating Strong Passwords and Using Password Managers

## *1.1 What Makes a Strong Password?*

A strong password is one that is difficult for attackers to guess or crack. A weak password, such as "123456" or "password," can be easily cracked using brute-force methods, where an attacker systematically attempts all possible combinations. To create a strong password, consider the following factors:

1. **Length:**

- o The longer the password, the harder it is to crack. A password should be at least **12-16 characters** long. Each additional character increases the number of possible combinations exponentially.
- o **Example:** "B3autiful$&Day99" is a strong, long password compared to a simple "qwerty123".

2. **Complexity:**

- o Use a combination of **uppercase letters**, **lowercase letters**, **numbers**, and **special characters** (e.g., !, @, #, $, %, &).
- o **Example:** "M!cRo$2Rav@99" is much harder to guess than "password123."

3. **Avoid Personal Information:**

- o Refrain from using easily guessable information, such as names, birthdays, or common words. Personal information like your pet's name or family members' birthdays are common guesses for attackers.
- o **Example:** Avoid using passwords like "JohnDoe1990" or "Summer2021."

4. **Unpredictability:**

- o Use random strings of characters rather than predictable patterns (e.g., "abc123" or "password").

- o **Example:** Use passphrases with random words or an unrecognizable combination of characters: "Purple@Rabbit$F1shT!me."

5. **Passphrases:**

   - o A passphrase is a sequence of random words combined into a long, memorable string. It is easier to remember and still provides high security.
   - o **Example:** "Turtle$Dance!Banana!23" is easier to remember and still strong.

## *1.2 Using Password Managers*

Managing strong, unique passwords for every account can be difficult, especially when the number of online services grows. **Password managers** provide a secure solution by storing all your passwords in an encrypted vault. These tools generate, store, and autofill complex passwords for you, ensuring that each account has a unique, hard-to-guess password.

**Advantages of Using a Password Manager:**

- **Generate Strong Passwords:** Password managers can create highly complex and random passwords, ensuring that each account has a different, secure password.
- **Encryption:** Password managers encrypt your password vault with a master password, protecting your data even if the manager itself is compromised.

- **Convenience:** Password managers make it easy to access your passwords securely without having to remember or write them down.

## Popular Password Managers:

- **LastPass:** A widely used password manager that provides strong encryption and easy password generation and storage.
- **1Password:** Known for its security features and user-friendly interface.
- **Bitwarden:** An open-source password manager that offers a free plan with strong security features.
- **Dashlane:** Provides advanced security features such as dark web monitoring in addition to password storage.

## How to Use a Password Manager:

- Choose a password manager that fits your needs and platform.
- Set up your account with a **strong master password**.
- Use the manager's built-in password generator to create strong, unique passwords for each account.
- Enable **two-factor authentication (2FA)** for an added layer of security on the password manager itself.

## 2. The Importance of Password Hygiene and Policies for Businesses

### 2.1 Password Hygiene for Individuals

**Password hygiene** refers to the practices and habits that individuals adopt to maintain the security of their passwords. Good password hygiene reduces the risk of unauthorized access and minimizes the impact of a potential breach.

1. **Never Reuse Passwords:**
   - Using the same password across multiple accounts increases the risk of a breach. If one account is compromised, all other accounts using the same password are vulnerable.
   - **Best Practice:** Use a unique password for every account.

2. **Change Passwords Regularly:**
   - While modern systems do not require frequent changes, it's still a good practice to update passwords for critical accounts periodically, especially if you suspect a breach.
   - **Best Practice:** Change passwords for banking, email, and social media accounts every few months.

3. **Monitor Account Activity:**
   - Regularly review the activity on your accounts to detect any unusual or unauthorized access.

o **Best Practice:** Enable **security alerts** for account logins, password changes, and other important activities.

4. **Avoid Using Public Wi-Fi for Sensitive Transactions:**

o Avoid logging into sensitive accounts (e.g., banking) over public Wi-Fi networks, as attackers can intercept data transmitted over unsecured networks.

o **Best Practice:** Use a **VPN** (Virtual Private Network) when accessing accounts over public Wi-Fi.

## *2.2 Password Policies for Businesses*

For businesses, implementing strong **password policies** is essential to protect organizational data and prevent unauthorized access to critical systems. A well-defined password policy helps ensure that employees follow best practices for password creation, management, and use.

1. **Enforce Strong Password Creation Rules:**

o Organizations should require employees to create passwords that meet specific criteria, such as minimum length, complexity (upper and lowercase letters, numbers, special characters), and non-reuse across multiple systems.

o **Example Policy:** Passwords must be at least 12 characters long and contain at least one uppercase letter, one lowercase letter, one number, and one special character.

2. **Mandate Regular Password Changes:**
   o While overzealous password expiration policies can lead to weak passwords, it's important to enforce periodic changes for critical systems and sensitive accounts.
   o **Example Policy:** Require users to change passwords every 90 days for systems containing sensitive information (e.g., financial systems, HR data).

3. **Implement MFA for Critical Accounts:**
   o Require multi-factor authentication (MFA) for all accounts that have access to sensitive company data or systems. This adds an additional layer of security in case passwords are compromised.
   o **Example Policy:** Enforce MFA on all employee email accounts and cloud-based applications like customer relationship management (CRM) systems.

4. **Establish a Password Manager Requirement:**
   o Encourage or require employees to use a password manager for storing and managing company-related passwords. This helps ensure that passwords are strong, unique, and securely stored.

- o **Example Policy:** Employees must use a company-approved password manager to store their passwords, which should also be encrypted.

5. **Educate Employees on Password Security:**
   - o Regularly train employees on the importance of password security, how to create strong passwords, and how to avoid common mistakes (e.g., phishing attacks or password reuse).
   - o **Example Policy:** Conduct annual cybersecurity awareness training that includes best practices for password management and recognizing phishing attacks.

6. **Monitor and Audit Access:**
   - o Continuously monitor and audit the use of passwords, access to critical systems, and login attempts to detect any suspicious activity.
   - o **Example Policy:** Implement a **password breach alert system** that flags attempts to log in with incorrect passwords multiple times or from unknown devices or locations.

# 3. Best Practices for Maintaining Strong Password Security

1. **Use Multi-Factor Authentication (MFA) Everywhere Possible:**

   o In addition to strong passwords, always enable MFA for an added layer of security, especially on accounts that contain sensitive information or provide access to critical systems.

2. **Ensure Security of Password Storage:**

   o Never store passwords in plain text files or unencrypted systems. Use password managers to securely store passwords and ensure encryption.

3. **Monitor for Leaked Credentials:**

   o Regularly check if your accounts have been part of a data breach using services like **Have I Been Pwned**. If an account is compromised, immediately change the password and implement MFA.

4. **Encourage Employees to Avoid Password Sharing:**

   o Discourage sharing passwords with coworkers or third parties. Instead, provide shared access mechanisms like **shared folders, role-based access control**, or **single sign-on (SSO)** to ensure security while providing access to necessary resources.

Password security is a cornerstone of cybersecurity, and it is vital for individuals and businesses to implement strong, unique passwords and effective password management practices. Using password managers, enforcing complex password policies, and combining strong passwords with multi-factor authentication (MFA) can significantly reduce the risk of unauthorized access to sensitive information. By fostering a culture of good password hygiene and enforcing security policies, businesses can minimize the risk of data breaches, enhance operational security, and protect against evolving cyber threats.

# Chapter 20: Building a Cybersecurity Policy for Your Organization

## *Overview*

A **cybersecurity policy** is a crucial document that defines the framework, guidelines, and strategies for protecting an organization's information systems, networks, and data from cyber threats. It provides employees, contractors, and other stakeholders with a clear understanding of how to manage and protect sensitive information. Developing a robust cybersecurity policy is essential for safeguarding against attacks, ensuring compliance with regulatory requirements, and maintaining business continuity. This chapter outlines the steps for developing a cybersecurity policy and key components to include in an organization's cybersecurity framework.

---

## 1. How to Develop a Robust Cybersecurity Policy

### *1.1 Understand the Organizational Needs*

Before creating a cybersecurity policy, it's essential to understand the specific needs and risks of the organization. This involves assessing the organization's infrastructure, business processes, and types of data it handles.

- **Conduct a Risk Assessment:** Identify potential threats (e.g., hacking, insider threats, data breaches) and vulnerabilities (e.g., outdated software, weak passwords). Understand the potential impact of a cyberattack on the organization.

- **Consider Legal and Regulatory Requirements:** Different industries are subject to specific cybersecurity regulations (e.g., **GDPR, HIPAA, PCI-DSS**). Ensure that the policy aligns with legal compliance requirements.

### *1.2 Define the Scope and Objectives of the Policy*

A well-defined policy should outline the scope of cybersecurity efforts within the organization and set clear objectives for protection. The policy should be broad enough to cover all aspects of the organization's operations but specific enough to address its unique risks.

- **Key Objectives:**
  - Protecting sensitive data (e.g., financial records, employee information).
  - Maintaining the confidentiality, integrity, and availability of systems and networks.
  - Ensuring business continuity in case of a cybersecurity incident.
  - Complying with relevant laws, regulations, and standards.

## *1.3 Involve Stakeholders*

The development of a cybersecurity policy should not be done in isolation. Involve key stakeholders from different departments (e.g., IT, legal, HR, and finance) to ensure the policy is comprehensive and considers all organizational needs.

- **Example:** Collaboration with the HR department is crucial for addressing employee access controls and training, while the legal team ensures that the policy complies with industry regulations.

## *1.4 Develop Clear, Actionable Guidelines*

Cybersecurity policies should be practical and easy to follow. Create specific guidelines and procedures that employees can understand and follow to reduce risks.

- **Actionable Guidelines:**
    - Guidelines for creating strong passwords and using multi-factor authentication (MFA).
    - Protocols for handling sensitive data, including encryption and access controls.
    - Procedures for reporting security incidents or breaches.

## *1.5 Regularly Review and Update the Policy*

Cybersecurity is an evolving field, with new threats and technologies emerging regularly. Therefore, it is essential to review and update the cybersecurity policy periodically to ensure it stays relevant and effective.

- **Best Practice:** Schedule regular reviews of the policy—at least annually or after significant changes to the organization's infrastructure or external threat landscape.

## 2. Key Components to Include in an Organization's Cybersecurity Framework

A comprehensive cybersecurity policy should address various aspects of an organization's cybersecurity needs, from risk management and incident response to data protection and employee training. Below are the key components that should be included:

### 2.1 Information Security Policy

This section should outline the organization's approach to securing its information systems and sensitive data. It sets the foundation for protecting digital assets and sensitive information, both in storage and in transit.

- **Key Areas:**
  - Data classification and handling procedures (e.g., how to label, store, and dispose of sensitive data).
  - Encryption protocols for data at rest and in transit.

o Guidelines for accessing and sharing data internally and externally.

## 2.2 Access Control Policy

Access control defines who can access certain resources and how their access is granted, monitored, and revoked. It should enforce the **principle of least privilege** (PoLP), ensuring that users have only the minimum level of access required for their roles.

- **Key Areas:**
    - o Role-based access control (RBAC) or attribute-based access control (ABAC).
    - o Multi-factor authentication (MFA) requirements for accessing critical systems.
    - o Procedures for granting, changing, and revoking access rights for employees and contractors.

## 2.3 Network Security Policy

This section outlines how the organization's networks (internal, external, and cloud-based) are protected against unauthorized access, data breaches, and attacks like DDoS (Distributed Denial of Service).

- **Key Areas:**
    - o Network perimeter security measures (e.g., firewalls, intrusion detection/prevention systems).
    - o Secure remote access protocols, such as VPNs (Virtual Private Networks).

    o   Network monitoring and logging for detecting unauthorized access.

## 2.4 Endpoint Security Policy

Endpoint devices such as desktops, laptops, and mobile devices are often targets for cyberattacks. This policy should define how these devices are secured to prevent malicious software, unauthorized access, and data breaches.

- **Key Areas:**
  - o Device encryption and secure boot options.
  - o Anti-malware software deployment and updates.
  - o Mobile device management (MDM) for securing and remotely wiping lost or stolen devices.

## 2.5 Incident Response and Recovery Plan

An incident response plan (IRP) outlines how the organization will detect, respond to, and recover from cybersecurity incidents (e.g., data breaches, ransomware attacks).

- **Key Areas:**
  - o Incident detection and reporting procedures.
  - o Designating an incident response team and outlining their roles and responsibilities.
  - o Post-incident analysis and reporting to identify the root cause and prevent future incidents.

## *2.6 Disaster Recovery and Business Continuity Plan*

A disaster recovery (DR) and business continuity (BC) plan ensures that the organization can quickly recover from major disruptions caused by cyberattacks, natural disasters, or system failures.

- **Key Areas:**
  - Backup and recovery procedures for critical data and systems.
  - Defined recovery time objectives (RTO) and recovery point objectives (RPO) for key business functions.
  - Communication protocols to inform employees, customers, and stakeholders about system outages or security breaches.

## *2.7 Employee Awareness and Training Policy*

A key element of any cybersecurity policy is employee education. Human error is often a significant factor in security incidents, so training employees on security best practices is essential.

- **Key Areas:**
  - Regular cybersecurity awareness training (e.g., phishing prevention, safe use of passwords).
  - Simulated phishing campaigns to test employee awareness.

   o   Reporting procedures for suspicious activities or
       security incidents.

## 2.8 Physical Security Policy

Physical security measures help prevent unauthorized access to
critical infrastructure, such as servers, network equipment, and data
centers.

- **Key Areas:**
  - o Secure access to physical spaces (e.g., card access
      systems, biometric scanning).
  - o Guidelines for handling hardware or storage devices
      (e.g., laptops, USB drives) that may contain sensitive
      information.
  - o Procedures for the destruction of physical data
      storage media, such as hard drives and paper records.

## 2.9 Compliance and Legal Considerations

Organizations must comply with various regulations, industry
standards, and legal requirements regarding data protection, privacy,
and cybersecurity.

- **Key Areas:**
  - o Compliance with standards like **GDPR**, **HIPAA**,
      **PCI-DSS**, and **SOX**.
  - o Regular audits to ensure adherence to these
      regulations.

o   Legal consequences for non-compliance with data protection laws.

---

## 3.

Building a robust cybersecurity policy is essential for safeguarding an organization's digital assets, protecting sensitive data, and ensuring business continuity in the event of a cyberattack or data breach. A well-structured cybersecurity policy addresses all aspects of an organization's operations, from user access management and network security to incident response and employee training. By incorporating key components such as access control, incident response, disaster recovery, and compliance, organizations can establish a comprehensive framework to mitigate cyber risks and protect against evolving threats. Regularly reviewing and updating the cybersecurity policy ensures that it remains relevant and effective in an ever-changing threat landscape.

# Chapter 21: Employee Training and Awareness

*Overview*

Cybersecurity threats are constantly evolving, and employees remain one of the most critical factors in defending against cyberattacks. Human error is often the weakest link in an organization's cybersecurity chain, whether due to lack of awareness, negligence, or falling victim to social engineering tactics. **Employee cybersecurity awareness training** is essential for reducing risks, improving security posture, and ensuring that employees understand their role in protecting sensitive data and systems. This chapter explores the importance of cybersecurity awareness training, common phishing scams, and how employees can avoid falling victim to them.

## 1. The Importance of Cybersecurity Awareness Training for Employees

### 1.1 Human Error and the Role of Employees in Cybersecurity

While advanced technical tools, firewalls, and encryption can help protect systems, employees are often the first line of defense. Human error, such as clicking on malicious links, using weak passwords, or mishandling sensitive data, is a significant contributor to security breaches.

- **Example:** An employee inadvertently sends an email with sensitive information to the wrong recipient or falls for a phishing scam, giving hackers access to company systems.

The goal of cybersecurity awareness training is to educate employees about potential threats, empower them to identify security risks, and instill a culture of security-conscious behavior.

### *1.2 Reducing the Risk of Cybersecurity Incidents*

Cybersecurity awareness training helps to significantly reduce the likelihood of successful attacks, such as phishing, ransomware, and social engineering. By providing employees with the knowledge and skills to recognize threats and respond appropriately, organizations can improve their overall security posture.

**Benefits of Employee Training:**

- **Identifying Threats Early:** Training employees to recognize phishing emails, suspicious links, and other potential threats enables them to act quickly and minimize the impact of cyberattacks.
- **Improved Response to Security Incidents:** Trained employees know the correct procedures for reporting

incidents and escalating issues to the appropriate security teams.

- **Regulatory Compliance:** Many industries require organizations to provide cybersecurity training to comply with data protection regulations (e.g., GDPR, HIPAA). Regular training helps organizations meet these compliance requirements.

## *1.3 Creating a Security-Conscious Culture*

Cybersecurity awareness training fosters a **security-conscious culture** within an organization, where employees are proactive about safeguarding information, report suspicious activities, and adhere to company security policies. When cybersecurity becomes part of the organizational culture, employees are more likely to take personal responsibility for securing their work and personal devices.

- **Example:** In a security-conscious culture, employees routinely update their passwords, avoid using the same passwords for multiple accounts, and implement multi-factor authentication (MFA) where possible.

## *1.4 Ongoing and Dynamic Training Programs*

Cybersecurity threats evolve, and so should employee training programs. Ongoing, dynamic training ensures employees are kept up-to-date on the latest threats and best practices for preventing them.

- **Best Practice:** Conduct regular refresher training and simulations to test employees' responses to new threats, such as the latest phishing scams or ransomware tactics.

## 2. Common Phishing Scams and How to Avoid Them

Phishing is one of the most common and effective social engineering tactics used by cybercriminals. It involves tricking individuals into revealing sensitive information, such as login credentials, financial data, or personal details, often through email or fake websites. Training employees to recognize phishing scams is critical to preventing data breaches and financial loss.

### 2.1 What is Phishing?

Phishing is a fraudulent attempt to obtain sensitive information by disguising as a trustworthy entity. It is often carried out through email, but phishing can also occur via text messages (smishing) or phone calls (vishing).

Phishing attacks typically involve:

- **Urgent Requests:** The attacker creates a sense of urgency, such as claiming that the recipient's account will be locked unless they take immediate action.
- **Fake Websites:** Attackers often direct the victim to a fake website that looks almost identical to a legitimate one, where

the victim is prompted to enter login credentials or other personal information.

- **Malicious Attachments or Links:** Emails may contain links or attachments that, when clicked, lead to malware downloads or direct users to fake login pages.

## 2.2 Types of Phishing Scams

1. **Email Phishing:**
   - The most common form of phishing, where attackers send emails impersonating legitimate entities, such as banks, government agencies, or internal company departments, to trick users into revealing sensitive information.
   - **Example:** An email that looks like it's from your bank asks you to click a link to verify your account information, but the link leads to a fake site designed to steal your credentials.

2. **Spear Phishing:**
   - Unlike general phishing, spear phishing is a targeted attack aimed at specific individuals or organizations. Attackers often gather personal information about the victim to create a more convincing email.
   - **Example:** A spear-phishing email might be sent to an executive, impersonating a colleague, and asking

the executive to wire money to a fraudulent bank account.

3. **Whaling:**
   - Whaling is a type of spear phishing that targets high-profile individuals, such as executives, board members, or other decision-makers, often for financial gain.
   - **Example:** A fake email from a supplier asking the CEO to approve an urgent transfer of funds.

4. **Smishing (SMS Phishing):**
   - Phishing that occurs through text messages (SMS). The message typically contains a link that leads to a fake website or prompts the user to download a malicious app.
   - **Example:** A text message claiming to be from a bank, telling the recipient that their account is at risk and asking them to click a link to verify their identity.

5. **Vishing (Voice Phishing):**
   - Phishing attacks carried out over the phone, where the attacker pretends to be a legitimate organization, such as a bank or government agency, and tries to trick the victim into providing sensitive information.
   - **Example:** A phone call from someone claiming to be from tech support, asking for remote access to the victim's computer.

## 2.3 Red Flags of Phishing Scams

Phishing emails and messages often have warning signs that employees can learn to identify. Some common red flags include:

- **Generic Greetings:** Phishing emails often use generic salutations like "Dear Customer" or "Dear User" instead of addressing you by name.
- **Suspicious Links:** Hovering over a link often reveals a different URL than the one displayed in the email. Avoid clicking on any link or downloading attachments if you are unsure of the sender's identity.
- **Spelling and Grammar Errors:** Phishing emails often contain spelling mistakes or awkward phrasing that legitimate companies would typically avoid.
- **Urgent or Threatening Language:** Phishing emails often create a sense of urgency by threatening account suspension, asking for immediate payment, or warning of a security breach.
- **Unknown Senders:** Be cautious of emails from unknown or unexpected sources, especially if they contain attachments or links.

## 2.4 How to Avoid Phishing Scams

1. **Verify the Source:**

o Always verify the source of any unexpected email or message. Contact the company or organization directly using known contact information (e.g., phone number or official website) instead of clicking on links or replying to the message.

2. **Use Multi-Factor Authentication (MFA):**

   o Enabling MFA adds an extra layer of protection, so even if login credentials are compromised, the attacker still cannot access the account without the second authentication factor (e.g., SMS code or authentication app).

3. **Do Not Click on Suspicious Links or Open Unknown Attachments:**

   o Be cautious with emails containing links or attachments. If the email appears suspicious, do not click the links or open attachments, especially if you weren't expecting them.

4. **Educate and Train Employees Regularly:**

   o Ongoing training is crucial for keeping employees informed about the latest phishing techniques and how to recognize them. Regular phishing simulations can also help test their knowledge and response.

5. **Use Email Filtering and Anti-Phishing Software:**

   o Implement email filtering software that can automatically flag or block potential phishing emails.

Anti-phishing tools can also help identify malicious websites or links.

6. **Report Suspected Phishing Attempts:**
   o If an employee suspects they've received a phishing email, they should immediately report it to the IT or security team, who can take appropriate action, such as blocking the sender or scanning for malware.

---

## 3.

Employee cybersecurity awareness training is a fundamental part of a robust security strategy. By educating employees about common cyber threats, such as phishing scams, and equipping them with the knowledge to recognize and avoid these threats, organizations can significantly reduce the risk of a successful attack. Training employees to follow best practices, such as using multi-factor authentication (MFA), verifying suspicious messages, and reporting potential threats, empowers them to be proactive defenders of their company's digital assets. Regular training and phishing simulations ensure that employees stay vigilant and prepared, ultimately strengthening the organization's overall cybersecurity posture.

# Chapter 22: Incident Response and Recovery

## Overview

A cyberattack can strike unexpectedly, potentially causing significant damage to an organization's systems, data, and reputation. Having a well-defined **Incident Response (IR)** and **Recovery** plan in place is crucial to effectively handle a cyberattack and minimize its impact. This chapter outlines the steps organizations should take to prepare for a cyberattack, how to respond efficiently during an incident, and the steps involved in recovery and incident management.

---

## 1. How to Prepare for and Respond to a Cyberattack

### 1.1 Incident Response Planning

**Incident response planning** is a proactive approach to identifying, managing, and mitigating the effects of a cybersecurity incident. Preparing in advance helps organizations respond quickly and effectively to a cyberattack, minimizing the damage and downtime.

**Key Steps in Preparing for a Cyberattack:**

- **Define an Incident Response Team (IRT):** The **incident response team (IRT)** is responsible for coordinating the response to a cyberattack. The team should include members from various departments, including IT, legal, communications, and senior management.

- o **Team Roles:** Each member should have a clearly defined role. For example, the IT team might be responsible for technical response, while the legal team addresses compliance and regulatory concerns.
- **Develop an Incident Response Plan (IRP):** The **IRP** is a documented process that outlines how the organization will respond to various types of cybersecurity incidents. It should cover everything from initial detection to post-incident analysis.

  - o **Plan Components:** Incident identification, containment strategies, communication protocols, recovery procedures, and post-incident actions.
- **Identify Critical Assets and Data:** Assess your organization's systems, networks, and data to determine which are most critical to the business. This will help prioritize recovery efforts and focus resources on protecting the most vital assets.

  - o **Example:** Financial data, customer information, intellectual property, and operational systems may be considered high-priority assets.
- **Set up Detection and Monitoring Tools:** Implement monitoring systems to detect suspicious activity, potential

vulnerabilities, and actual breaches. Intrusion Detection Systems (IDS), Security Information and Event Management (SIEM) systems, and endpoint detection tools are useful for monitoring network traffic, user behavior, and system logs.

- o **Example:** An IDS can detect unusual traffic patterns that might indicate an ongoing cyberattack.
- **Conduct Regular Training and Simulations:** Regular training and simulated attacks (e.g., **red teaming**) help employees and the incident response team prepare for a real cyberattack. Simulations test the effectiveness of your incident response plan and improve coordination during an actual incident.
  - o **Example:** A simulated ransomware attack can help staff understand how to recognize phishing emails, isolate infected devices, and report issues to the IR team.

## 2. Steps Involved in Incident Management

When a cyberattack occurs, having a structured approach to managing the incident is critical for minimizing its impact. The incident response process can be broken down into several stages, each aimed at containing the attack, mitigating its effects, and restoring normal operations.

## *2.1 Detection and Identification*

The first step in responding to a cyberattack is detecting and identifying the incident as quickly as possible. Early detection minimizes the damage and allows the response team to react more effectively.

- **Signs of a Cyberattack:**
    - Unusual network traffic patterns or system behavior.
    - Alerts from intrusion detection/prevention systems.
    - Reports from employees or external partners regarding suspicious emails, activity, or access attempts.
- **Example:** A ransomware attack might be detected through alerts about encrypted files or abnormal file access.
- **Action:** When an incident is detected, the incident response team should verify whether the alert is legitimate, confirm the nature of the attack, and assess its scope.

## *2.2 Containment*

Once the incident is identified, the next step is to **contain** the attack to prevent it from spreading further across the organization's systems or networks.

- **Containment Strategies:**

- o **Short-Term Containment:** Disconnect affected systems from the network to stop the spread of malware or data theft. This may include disabling affected user accounts or blocking malicious IP addresses.

- o **Long-Term Containment:** Implement more comprehensive containment measures, such as isolating compromised systems, applying patches to prevent further exploitation, and monitoring affected areas for signs of escalation.

- **Example:** In a ransomware attack, isolating infected machines from the rest of the network and disabling file sharing can help prevent the spread of the ransomware to other devices.

## 2.3 Eradication

After containment, the next step is to **eradicate** the threat from your systems. This may involve removing malware, closing vulnerabilities, and eliminating any backdoors or unauthorized access created by the attackers.

- **Eradication Methods:**
  - o Remove malicious files or software.
  - o Patch vulnerabilities or misconfigurations that were exploited during the attack.
  - o Reset compromised credentials or access keys.

- **Example:** After isolating a ransomware infection, removing the malicious code, restoring deleted files from backups, and updating software vulnerabilities are essential to ensure the attack is fully eradicated.

## 2.4 Recovery

Once the threat has been eradicated, the organization can begin the process of **recovery**—restoring systems, data, and services to normal operation while ensuring that security measures are in place to prevent future attacks.

- **Recovery Steps:**
    - **Restore from Backups:** If data loss occurred, use secure, uninfected backups to restore systems and files.
    - **Test Systems and Networks:** Test the integrity of recovered systems and networks to ensure they are functioning normally and that the threat has been completely eliminated.
    - **Gradual Restoration:** Reconnect systems to the network in a controlled manner, starting with critical systems and gradually restoring less critical services.
- **Example:** After restoring a compromised file server from backup, run antivirus and malware scans to ensure it's free of any remaining threats before reconnecting it to the network.

## *2.5 Communication*

Throughout the entire incident response process, **communication** is crucial to ensure that all stakeholders are informed and that the organization can respond effectively.

- **Internal Communication:** Ensure that the incident response team is in constant communication throughout the process. Keep key internal stakeholders, such as executives and department heads, informed about the situation and recovery progress.

- **External Communication:** Depending on the severity of the attack, the organization may need to communicate with customers, vendors, and the public. This may include notifying affected parties about data breaches, working with law enforcement, and issuing public statements.
  - **Example:** In the case of a data breach involving customer information, the organization must notify affected individuals and, if applicable, regulatory bodies such as **GDPR** under the required timeframes.

## *2.6 Post-Incident Analysis*

After the attack has been contained and systems are restored, it's essential to conduct a **post-incident analysis** to assess the effectiveness of the response and learn from the incident.

- **Review the Response:** Evaluate how well the incident response plan worked, whether the correct procedures were followed, and where improvements can be made.

- **Identify Vulnerabilities:** Determine how the attack occurred and identify any gaps in your cybersecurity defenses or incident response strategy.

- **Report and Document:** Document the details of the attack, the organization's response, and the lessons learned. This documentation is critical for compliance purposes and future reference.

- **Example:** A post-incident review might identify that the attack originated from a phishing email that bypassed email filtering, leading to changes in email filtering rules and employee training on phishing.

---

Cyberattacks are an inevitable risk in today's digital world, and organizations must be prepared to handle them swiftly and effectively. A robust incident response plan (IRP) that includes preparation, detection, containment, eradication, recovery, and communication can significantly reduce the damage caused by cyberattacks. Regularly reviewing and updating the response plan, conducting simulated attacks, and educating employees on recognizing threats are key to ensuring organizational resilience. Following a structured approach to incident management, organizations can not only minimize the impact of cyberattacks but also recover quickly and strengthen their cybersecurity posture against future threats.

# Chapter 23: Penetration Testing and Vulnerability Assessment

*Overview*

In today's cybersecurity landscape, organizations face a wide array of threats from hackers, cybercriminals, and insiders. Proactively identifying and addressing vulnerabilities is crucial to safeguarding systems, networks, and sensitive data. **Penetration testing** and **vulnerability assessments** are two critical techniques used to discover weaknesses in an organization's infrastructure before attackers can exploit them. This chapter explores the role of penetration testing in identifying weaknesses, how vulnerability assessments help improve security measures, and the best practices for implementing both strategies.

## 1. The Role of Penetration Testing in Identifying Weaknesses

*1.1 What is Penetration Testing?*

Penetration testing, also known as **ethical hacking**, is a simulated cyberattack performed by cybersecurity professionals to identify vulnerabilities in a system, network, or application. The goal of penetration testing is to mimic the tactics, techniques, and procedures (TTPs) used by real-world attackers to uncover weaknesses before malicious hackers can exploit them.

Penetration testers, often referred to as **white-hat hackers**, use various tools and methodologies to exploit potential vulnerabilities and assess the security posture of the system.

- **Example:** A penetration test might involve attempting to exploit known vulnerabilities in a web application or network infrastructure, such as SQL injection or cross-site scripting (XSS), to gain unauthorized access and see what information can be retrieved.

### 1.2 Types of Penetration Testing

Penetration testing can be conducted in several different ways, depending on the scope and the systems being tested. These include:

1. **External Penetration Testing:**
   o Focuses on testing the security of external-facing systems, such as websites, email servers, and other public-facing applications. The tester simulates an attack from an external hacker trying to breach the system from the internet.
2. **Internal Penetration Testing:**
   o Simulates an attack from an insider, such as a disgruntled employee or someone who has already gained access to the organization's internal network.

This test helps identify risks that might exist within the internal infrastructure.

3. **Web Application Penetration Testing:**
   - Focuses on identifying vulnerabilities in web applications, such as SQL injection, cross-site scripting (XSS), and broken authentication. This type of testing is crucial for organizations that provide web-based services.

4. **Social Engineering Penetration Testing:**
   - Involves attempting to manipulate employees into revealing sensitive information, such as passwords, or taking actions that could lead to a security breach (e.g., clicking on phishing emails or providing access to restricted areas).

*1.3 Penetration Testing Methodology*

Penetration testers follow a structured methodology to ensure that all potential attack vectors are tested thoroughly. The typical phases of a penetration test include:

1. **Planning and Reconnaissance:**
   - **Objective:** Gather information about the target system. This includes domain names, IP addresses, software versions, and network topology.

o **Example:** An attacker might use tools like **WHOIS** or **Shodan** to gather public information about the target system.

2. **Scanning:**

   o **Objective:** Scan the system for open ports, services, and vulnerabilities that may be exploited. This step often involves using automated vulnerability scanning tools.

   o **Example:** Tools like **Nmap** or **Nessus** can be used to scan for open ports and known vulnerabilities.

3. **Gaining Access:**

   o **Objective:** Attempt to exploit identified vulnerabilities to gain unauthorized access to the system. This phase might involve techniques such as exploiting weak passwords, injection attacks, or exploiting outdated software.

   o **Example:** Exploiting a SQL injection vulnerability to access the backend database of a website.

4. **Maintaining Access:**

   o **Objective:** Simulate how an attacker would establish a persistent presence in the system to maintain control. This step tests how well the organization can detect and mitigate continuous threats.

   o **Example:** Installing a backdoor to maintain access after the initial breach.

5. **Analysis and Reporting:**

  o **Objective:** After the test is completed, penetration testers compile findings and provide a report to the organization. This includes details about the vulnerabilities discovered, how they were exploited, and recommendations for mitigating them.

  o **Example:** A report might highlight the exploitation of an outdated web server and recommend patching it or upgrading to a more secure version.

---

# 2. How Vulnerability Assessments Help Improve Security Measures

### 2.1 What is a Vulnerability Assessment?

A **vulnerability assessment** is the process of systematically identifying, quantifying, and prioritizing vulnerabilities in a system or network. Unlike penetration testing, which involves actively exploiting vulnerabilities, vulnerability assessments focus on scanning for known vulnerabilities and weaknesses.

A vulnerability assessment provides an overview of the security posture of the organization, helping IT teams prioritize fixes based on the severity and potential impact of the vulnerabilities identified.

- **Example:** A vulnerability scan might identify outdated software with known vulnerabilities (e.g., an unpatched operating system) or misconfigurations (e.g., open ports on firewalls that should be closed).

## *2.2 Vulnerability Assessment vs. Penetration Testing*

While both penetration testing and vulnerability assessments aim to identify weaknesses, they differ in their approach and scope:

- **Penetration Testing:** Involves actively exploiting vulnerabilities to simulate a real-world cyberattack. It focuses on the attacker's perspective, attempting to gain access to sensitive information or systems.
- **Vulnerability Assessment:** Focuses on scanning for and identifying known vulnerabilities without actively exploiting them. It provides a broader view of security issues and helps prioritize patches and fixes based on the severity of vulnerabilities.

### Benefits of Vulnerability Assessments:

- **Broad Coverage:** Vulnerability assessments scan the entire network and systems for a wide range of potential vulnerabilities, from outdated software to misconfigurations.
- **Continuous Monitoring:** Vulnerability assessments can be scheduled regularly (e.g., weekly or monthly) to ensure

systems are always checked for newly discovered vulnerabilities.

- **Risk Prioritization:** Once vulnerabilities are identified, they can be categorized based on risk levels (e.g., high, medium, low), helping IT teams focus on the most critical issues first.

## *2.3 Steps in Conducting a Vulnerability Assessment*

1. **Asset Identification:**
   - o The first step is to identify and catalog the assets within the organization, including hardware, software, networks, and applications.
   - o **Example:** Creating an inventory of all servers, workstations, cloud applications, and networking devices.

2. **Vulnerability Scanning:**
   - o Using automated tools (e.g., **Nessus, OpenVAS, Qualys**) to scan systems for known vulnerabilities, misconfigurations, and outdated software.
   - o **Example:** Scanning for outdated software with known vulnerabilities, such as a web server running an outdated version of Apache with an unpatched bug.

3. **Risk Assessment and Prioritization:**

- o Once vulnerabilities are identified, they are assessed for risk based on factors such as potential impact, exploitability, and the criticality of the affected system.
- o **Example:** A vulnerability in a public-facing website is considered more critical than one in an internal non-production server.

4. **Reporting and Recommendations:**
   - o A comprehensive report is generated, listing vulnerabilities, their severity, and recommended remediation steps (e.g., patching software, closing open ports, improving access controls).
   - o **Example:** The report might recommend updating the web server software, restricting access to certain network resources, or implementing stronger password policies.

# 3. Penetration Testing and Vulnerability Assessment Best Practices

1. **Conduct Regular Assessments:**
   - o Organizations should regularly conduct both vulnerability assessments and penetration tests to ensure their systems are secure. Regular assessments

help identify new vulnerabilities that could arise from software updates or system changes.

2. **Use Automated Tools and Manual Testing:**

   o  While automated vulnerability scanning tools are essential, combining them with manual testing ensures a more comprehensive security assessment. Penetration testers can uncover vulnerabilities that automated tools might miss, such as logic flaws or complex attack vectors.

3. **Remediate Quickly:**

   o  After identifying vulnerabilities, it is critical to fix them as soon as possible. Prioritize vulnerabilities based on their severity and potential impact, and implement fixes or patches without delay.

4. **Test Critical Systems First:**

   o  When conducting penetration testing or vulnerability assessments, start with the most critical systems, such as those that handle sensitive data or critical business functions.

5. **Simulate Real-World Attacks:**

   o  When conducting penetration testing, try to simulate the tactics, techniques, and procedures (TTPs) of real-world attackers. This will provide a more accurate assessment of how well your systems can withstand actual cyberattacks.

Penetration testing and vulnerability assessments are two essential tools in any organization's cybersecurity strategy. Penetration testing provides a simulated attack to identify exploitable weaknesses, while vulnerability assessments offer a comprehensive scan for known vulnerabilities. By regularly conducting both, organizations can proactively identify and mitigate risks, strengthen their security posture, and better defend against the evolving threat landscape. Effective implementation of both strategies, along with swift remediation of identified vulnerabilities, is key to maintaining a secure and resilient infrastructure.

# Chapter 24: Advanced Threat Protection Tools

*Overview*

As cyber threats continue to grow in sophistication, traditional security methods often fall short of providing adequate protection. In response, **AI-driven threat detection** and **machine learning** (ML) technologies have emerged as powerful tools to help organizations proactively identify, prevent, and respond to advanced cyberattacks. These technologies not only enhance threat detection capabilities but also automate incident response, improving the overall efficiency of cybersecurity efforts. This chapter explores the role of AI and ML in transforming the landscape of cybersecurity and highlights key advanced threat protection tools.

## 1. Overview of AI-Driven Threat Detection and Response Tools

### *1.1 What is AI-Driven Threat Detection?*

AI-driven threat detection tools use machine learning algorithms and artificial intelligence to analyze vast amounts of data in real-time and identify patterns or anomalies that could indicate potential cyberattacks. Unlike traditional methods, which rely on predefined rules or signatures to detect threats, AI-driven tools can learn from data, adapt to new threats, and make decisions based on evolving patterns of behavior.

**How AI Enhances Threat Detection:**

- **Behavioral Analysis:** AI tools can analyze the behavior of users, devices, and applications across a network, identifying deviations from normal patterns that may indicate malicious activity.
  - ○ **Example:** An AI tool might detect unusual login attempts or unauthorized file access by identifying deviations from an employee's usual behavior.
- **Anomaly Detection:** AI can flag abnormal activity that might go unnoticed by traditional detection methods. This includes unusual traffic spikes, unauthorized changes to system configurations, or unexpected data movements.
  - ○ **Example:** An AI system might detect abnormal data exfiltration from an employee's device, signaling potential data theft.
- **Automated Analysis:** AI systems can automate the process of analyzing logs, network traffic, and security events, significantly reducing the time required to identify threats and improve the response speed.

*1.2 Key AI-Driven Threat Detection Tools*

Several AI-powered threat detection tools are used to protect organizations from cyberattacks. These tools often employ machine learning models to continuously adapt and improve their detection capabilities.

1. **CrowdStrike Falcon:**
   - A leading AI-driven endpoint protection tool, CrowdStrike Falcon uses machine learning to detect, prevent, and respond to security incidents on endpoints. It continuously analyzes endpoint data to identify malicious behaviors and automatically responds to threats in real-time.

2. **Darktrace:**
   - Darktrace is an AI-based cybersecurity platform that leverages machine learning to detect and respond to cyber threats across networks, cloud environments, and endpoints. Darktrace uses self-learning algorithms to understand the "pattern of life" of a network and identify deviations that may indicate potential threats, such as insider threats or advanced persistent threats (APTs).

3. **Cisco Secure Network Analytics:**
   - Cisco's solution uses machine learning and advanced analytics to detect, investigate, and respond to network threats. It uses AI to analyze network traffic and identify suspicious activities like data

exfiltration or command-and-control communication, helping organizations detect and mitigate threats more quickly.

4. **Vectra AI:**

   o Vectra uses AI and machine learning to provide threat detection and response across network traffic. It identifies hidden threats in real-time by analyzing network behavior and alerts security teams to anomalous patterns that may indicate cyberattacks.

5. **SentinelOne:**

   o SentinelOne's AI-driven platform provides endpoint protection and incident response. It uses behavioral AI to identify threats and automate remediation without human intervention, allowing it to quickly neutralize malware, ransomware, and other types of attacks.

# 2. How Machine Learning is Changing the Landscape of Cybersecurity

## 2.1 What is Machine Learning in Cybersecurity?

Machine learning (ML) is a subset of artificial intelligence that enables systems to learn from data, improve over time, and make decisions without being explicitly programmed. In cybersecurity, machine learning algorithms are used to detect, predict, and respond to a wide range of threats. Unlike traditional rule-based systems, machine learning algorithms can analyze large volumes of data to identify complex patterns and behaviors that may indicate a security threat.

**How Machine Learning Enhances Cybersecurity:**

- **Threat Detection and Classification:** ML models can classify threats based on historical data, categorizing them into different types such as phishing, malware, or insider threats. By training on labeled datasets of known attacks, machine learning systems can quickly identify new and evolving threats.
    - o **Example:** A machine learning model might be trained on historical phishing emails and then used to identify new phishing attempts in incoming messages.
- **Predictive Capabilities:** ML tools can predict future threats by analyzing trends and patterns in data, helping organizations proactively protect themselves before an attack occurs.
    - o **Example:** By analyzing historical attack patterns, machine learning systems can predict the likelihood of a targeted attack against an organization and suggest preventive measures.

- **Automated Response and Remediation:** Machine learning can be used to automate responses to security incidents, reducing the time between detection and response. Automated systems can take immediate action to mitigate threats without waiting for human intervention.
    - **Example:** In the case of a malware infection, a machine learning-based system could immediately isolate the affected endpoint, preventing further spread of the attack.

## 2.2 Types of Machine Learning in Cybersecurity

Machine learning in cybersecurity is applied in several areas, with different techniques being used to address specific challenges. Some common types of machine learning approaches include:

1. **Supervised Learning:**
    - In supervised learning, machine learning algorithms are trained on labeled datasets (i.e., data that has been pre-classified as either normal or malicious). This approach is useful for detecting known threats, such as malware signatures or specific attack patterns.
    - **Example:** Supervised learning algorithms might be trained on historical network traffic data to classify incoming traffic as either benign or suspicious.
2. **Unsupervised Learning:**

- o Unsupervised learning is used to detect anomalies and patterns in data without predefined labels. It's ideal for identifying new, unknown threats that have not been seen before.
- o **Example:** An unsupervised learning model might identify unusual behavior in a network, such as an unauthorized device communicating with critical infrastructure, even if the specific threat type has never been encountered.

3. **Reinforcement Learning:**
   - o In reinforcement learning, an agent learns to make decisions based on feedback from its actions. In the context of cybersecurity, reinforcement learning can be used to dynamically adjust defense strategies in response to changing attack tactics.
   - o **Example:** A reinforcement learning model could adapt its network defense techniques based on real-time feedback from ongoing attack simulations.

## *2.3 Benefits of Machine Learning in Cybersecurity*

1. **Improved Threat Detection:**
   - o Machine learning models can detect complex threats that might evade traditional security measures, such as zero-day vulnerabilities or advanced persistent threats (APTs). They do this by recognizing

abnormal patterns and behaviors in network traffic, application usage, and user activity.

2. **Faster Incident Response:**
   o ML can accelerate the detection and response process by automating tasks that would otherwise require human intervention. This helps organizations respond to threats more quickly and mitigate damage.

3. **Adaptive Defense Mechanisms:**
   o Machine learning algorithms continuously learn and adapt to new attack techniques. This makes it possible for cybersecurity tools to evolve and stay ahead of attackers, even as cyberattacks become more sophisticated.

4. **Proactive Threat Hunting:**
   o Machine learning systems can automatically scan for potential threats, even before an attack occurs. This proactive approach helps identify weak points and vulnerabilities in an organization's infrastructure.

## 3. Key AI-Driven Tools and Strategies for Threat Detection

1. **AI-Powered Firewalls:**
   o Next-generation firewalls with AI capabilities can analyze network traffic in real-time, using machine

learning to detect malicious activity based on patterns rather than predefined rules. These firewalls adapt and improve over time, becoming more efficient at identifying sophisticated threats.

2. **Endpoint Detection and Response (EDR):**
   o EDR platforms use machine learning to monitor endpoint activities and detect unusual behavior that could indicate a cyberattack. These platforms provide real-time alerts and allow security teams to investigate, isolate, and remediate threats.

3. **AI-Powered SIEM (Security Information and Event Management):**
   o AI-enhanced SIEM systems use machine learning to analyze vast amounts of security event data from various sources (e.g., logs, network traffic) to detect suspicious patterns and provide actionable insights for incident response.

4. **Threat Intelligence Platforms:**
   o AI and ML are used to analyze external threat intelligence data to predict emerging threats, track the activities of threat actors, and automate the process of integrating threat intelligence into security operations.

Machine learning and AI-driven tools are fundamentally transforming the landscape of cybersecurity by enabling organizations to detect, respond to, and mitigate threats more effectively. By leveraging advanced machine learning techniques, cybersecurity systems can detect complex threats, adapt to new attack vectors, and automate incident response, improving both security posture and operational efficiency. As cyber threats continue to evolve, incorporating AI and machine learning into cybersecurity strategies will be essential for staying ahead of malicious actors and ensuring that organizations remain secure in an increasingly digital world.

# Chapter 25: Staying Ahead: Future Trends in Cybersecurity

## *Overview*

As the digital world rapidly evolves, so do the methods and technologies used by cybercriminals. The landscape of cybersecurity is constantly changing, with new threats emerging alongside groundbreaking innovations. Staying ahead of these threats requires not only understanding current security challenges but also anticipating future trends and developments. In this chapter, we explore what the future holds for cybersecurity, focusing on emerging technologies such as **quantum computing** and **blockchain** and their potential impact on security practices.

---

## 1. What the Future Holds for Cybersecurity

### *1.1 The Growing Complexity of Cyber Threats*

Cyberattacks are becoming more sophisticated, with threat actors using advanced tactics such as artificial intelligence (AI), machine learning (ML), and automated tools to bypass traditional defenses. As organizations become more digitally connected and dependent on technology, the attack surface expands, providing more opportunities for cybercriminals to exploit vulnerabilities.

- **Example:** The rise of Internet of Things (IoT) devices has created an ever-growing number of entry points for attackers, as these devices often lack robust security measures and can be used as part of botnets in large-scale distributed denial-of-service (DDoS) attacks.

As cyber threats evolve, cybersecurity professionals must be able to anticipate these attacks, adapt security measures accordingly, and implement advanced detection and response systems that can react in real-time to emerging threats.

## *1.2 The Role of Automation and AI in Future Cybersecurity*

The increasing volume and complexity of cyber threats make manual detection and response impractical. As a result, automation and AI are expected to play an even greater role in cybersecurity in the future. Machine learning algorithms can be trained to identify threats based on patterns of behavior, while AI-driven systems can automatically mitigate risks and respond to attacks.

- **Example:** AI can be used for anomaly detection, recognizing unusual network traffic or behavior patterns that indicate a potential breach. Automated response tools could then quarantine compromised systems or block malicious activity without human intervention.

The future of cybersecurity will rely heavily on AI and automation to handle the scale and speed of emerging threats while ensuring a faster and more accurate response.

### 1.3 The Cybersecurity Skills Gap

Despite the growing demand for cybersecurity professionals, there is a significant skills gap in the industry. Organizations are struggling to find qualified personnel to protect their systems from evolving cyber threats. The future of cybersecurity will involve addressing this skills shortage through education, training, and the adoption of more automated systems that require less manual intervention.

- **Example:** Organizations may turn to AI-powered platforms to assist with monitoring, investigation, and incident response, thus allowing human security experts to focus on high-level strategy and decision-making.

### 1.4 Privacy and Data Protection in the Digital Future

With data breaches and privacy concerns on the rise, data protection will continue to be a top priority. The future of cybersecurity will involve not only securing systems but also ensuring that personal and organizational data is protected according to stricter regulatory standards. Emerging privacy technologies, such as **differential privacy** and **homomorphic encryption**, will play a key role in protecting data without sacrificing utility.

- **Example:** Privacy regulations like **GDPR** and **CCPA** will continue to shape how organizations handle and protect data, forcing businesses to implement robust encryption methods, access controls, and audit trails.

## 2. Emerging Technologies and Their Impact on Security

### *2.1 Quantum Computing and Cybersecurity*

Quantum computing represents a massive shift in computational power, with the potential to revolutionize everything from scientific research to encryption. While quantum computing offers immense benefits, it also poses significant risks to cybersecurity.

1. **Quantum Computing and Encryption:**
   - **Threat to Current Encryption Methods:** Many of today's encryption algorithms, such as RSA and ECC (Elliptic Curve Cryptography), rely on the difficulty of certain mathematical problems (e.g., factoring large numbers). Quantum computers, using **Shor's Algorithm**, could potentially solve these problems much faster than classical computers, rendering current encryption methods obsolete.
   - **Example:** A quantum computer could easily break the RSA encryption standard, which underpins much

of modern cybersecurity (including secure communication protocols like HTTPS).

2. **Quantum-Resistant Encryption:**

   o As quantum computers become more capable, researchers are developing **quantum-resistant** algorithms that rely on mathematical problems that are difficult for quantum computers to solve. The field of **post-quantum cryptography** aims to develop encryption systems that can withstand quantum computing power.

   o **Example:** Algorithms like **Lattice-based cryptography** are being studied for their potential to provide secure encryption even in a quantum world.

3. **Quantum Key Distribution (QKD):**

   o QKD is a technique that uses the principles of quantum mechanics to securely exchange cryptographic keys. QKD ensures that any attempt to intercept the communication will alter the quantum state of the key, making the attack detectable.

   o **Example:** Companies are already experimenting with QKD to create ultra-secure communications, which could eventually become a standard for high-security applications.

**Impact on Cybersecurity:** Quantum computing will likely disrupt current encryption standards, necessitating a shift toward quantum-resistant algorithms and the development of new cryptographic methods to secure communications and data.

## 2.2 Blockchain and Cybersecurity

Blockchain, the technology that underpins cryptocurrencies like Bitcoin, has shown significant potential for improving cybersecurity in various domains. Its decentralized and immutable nature makes it an ideal candidate for securing digital transactions, data integrity, and authentication systems.

1. **Blockchain for Secure Transactions:**
   o Blockchain's ability to securely record and verify transactions makes it an ideal solution for securing financial transactions, supply chain data, and identity management.
   o **Example:** Blockchain can ensure the integrity of financial transactions by providing a transparent and tamper-proof record of all interactions, making it difficult for attackers to manipulate the data.

2. **Blockchain for Identity Management:**
   o Blockchain can be used to create decentralized identity systems, where individuals control their personal data, reducing the risk of identity theft and unauthorized access.
   o **Example:** Instead of relying on centralized databases for storing sensitive information like

passwords, blockchain allows users to control access to their identity using private keys and smart contracts.

3. **Blockchain for Data Integrity and Auditing:**

   o Blockchain's immutability ensures that data, once recorded, cannot be altered or tampered with, which makes it ideal for maintaining the integrity of audit logs and historical data.

   o **Example:** Blockchain-based logging systems can be used to securely track and store logs of system activity, ensuring that they remain unaltered even in the case of a security breach.

4. **Smart Contracts for Automation:**

   o **Smart contracts** are self-executing contracts with the terms of the agreement directly written into code. These can be used to automate various processes within cybersecurity, such as network access control or incident response actions.

   o **Example:** In the event of a detected breach, a smart contract could automatically trigger certain predefined actions, such as isolating compromised systems or initiating a system-wide alert.

**Impact on Cybersecurity:** Blockchain's decentralized and immutable characteristics provide a strong foundation for secure transactions, identity management, and audit logging. The adoption of blockchain technology can significantly improve data integrity, transparency, and protection against unauthorized access.

---

The future of cybersecurity is shaped by the continuous evolution of technology and the growing sophistication of cyber threats. As new technologies like **quantum computing** and **blockchain** emerge, they bring both opportunities and challenges. Quantum computing presents a potential threat to existing encryption methods, requiring the development of new cryptographic algorithms, while blockchain offers promising solutions for securing transactions, enhancing data integrity, and managing digital identities.

To stay ahead of cybercriminals, organizations must continuously adapt to the changing cybersecurity landscape, leveraging emerging technologies to strengthen defenses and mitigate risks. By anticipating these future trends and proactively implementing cutting-edge technologies, businesses can better protect themselves against the ever-evolving threat landscape.

www.ingramcontent.com/pod-product-compliance
Lightning Source LLC
LaVergne TN
LVHW051319050326
832903LV00031B/3261